ATM & MPEG-2

Integrating Digital Video into Broadband Networks

Hewlett-Packard Professional Books

Atchison	Object-Oriented Test & Measurement Software Development in C++
Blinn	Portable Shell Programming: An Extensive Collection of Bourne Shell Examples
Blommers	Practical Planning for Network Growth
Caruso	Power Programming in HP OpenView: Developing CMIS Applications
Cook	Building Enterprise Information Architectures
Costa	Planning and Designing High Speed Networks Using 100VG-AnyLAN, Second Edition
Crane	A Simplified Approach to Image Processing: Classical and Modern Techniques
Day	The Color Scanning Handbook: Your Guide to Hewlett-Packard ScanJet Color Scanners
Fernandez	Configuring the Common Desktop Environment
Fristrup	USENET: Netnews for Everyone
Fristrup	The Essential Web Surfer Survival Guide
Grady	Practical Software Metrics for Project Management and Process Improvement
Grosvenor, Ichiro, O'Brien	Mainframe Downsizing to Upsize Your Business: IT-Preneuring
Gunn	A Guide to NetWare® for UNIX®
Helsel	Graphical Programming: A Tutorial for HP VEE
Helsel	Visual Programming with HP VEE, Second Edition
Holman, Lund	Instant JavaScript
Kane	PA-RISC 2.0 Architecture
Knouse	Practical DCE Programming
Lee	The ISDN Consultant: A Stress-Free Guide to High-Speed Communications
Lewis	The Art & Science of Smalltalk
Lund	Integrating UNIX® and PC Network Operating Systems
Madell	Disk and File Management Tasks on HP-UX
Mahoney	High-Mix Low-Volume Manufacturing
Malan, Letsinger, Coleman	Object-Oriented Development at Work: Fusion in the Real World
McFarland	X Windows on the World: Developing Internationalized Software with X, Motif®, and CDE
McMinds/Whitty	Writing Your Own OSF/Motif Widgets
Norton, DiPasquale	Thread Time: The Multithreaded Programming Guide
Orzessek, Sommer	ATM & MPEG-2: Integrating Digital Video Services into Broadband Networks
Phaal	LAN Traffic Management
Pipkin	Halting the Hacker: A Practical Guide to Computer Security
Poniatowski	The HP-UX System Administrator's "How To" Book
Poniatowski	HP-UX 10.x System Administration "How To" Book
Poniatowski	Learning the HP-UX Operating System
Poniatowski	The Windows NT and HP-UX System Administrator's How-To Book
Ryan	Distributed Object Technology: Concepts and Applications
Thomas	Cable Television Proof-of-Performance: A Practical Guide to Cable TV Compliance Measurements Using a Spectrum Analyzer
Weygant	Clusters for High Availability: A Primer of HP-UX Solutions
Witte	Electronic Test Instruments
Yawn, Stachnick, Sellars	The Legacy Continues: Using the HP 3000 with HP-UX and Windows NT

ATM & MPEG-2

Integrating Digital Video into Broadband Networks

Michael Orzessek and Peter Sommer
Hewlett-Packard Company

To join a Prentice Hall PTR Internet mailing list, point to:
http://www.prenhall.com/mail_lists/

Prentice Hall PTR
Upper Saddle River, NJ 07458
http://www.prenhall.com

Library of Congress Cataloging in Publication Data

Orzessek, Michael.
  ATM & MPEG-2 : integrating digital video into broadband networks /
Michael Orzessek and Peter Sommer.
     p.   cm. -- (Hewelett-Packard professional books)
  Includes index.
  ISBN 0-13-243700-7
  1. Digital television.   2. Asynchronous transfer mode. 3. Video
compression--Standards   I. Sommer, Peter.   II. Title.
III. Series.
  TK6678.079   1998
  621.388--dc2096   97-17365
                                                           CIP

Editorial/production supervision: *Craig Little*
Manufacturing manager: *Alexis R. Heydt*
Acquisitions editor: *Bernard Goodwin*
Marketing manager: *Miles Williams*
Editorial assistant: *Barbara Alfieri*
Cover design: *Scott Weiss*
Cover design director: *Jerry Votta*
Patricia Pekary, Manager Hewlett-Packard Press

 Published by Prentice Hall PTR
Prentice-Hall, Inc.
A Simon & Schuster Company
Upper Saddle River, New Jersey 07458

The publisher offers discounts on this book when ordered in bulk quantities.

For more information, contact Corporate Sales Department, Phone: 800-382-3419,
Fax: 201-236-7141; email: corpsales@prenhall.com or write: Corporate Sales
Department, Prentice Hall PTR, 1 Lake Street, Upper Saddle River, NJ 07458.

Prentice Hall books are widely used by corporations and government agencies for
training, marketing, and resale.

All product names mentioned herein are the trademarks of their respective owners.

Portions Copyright 1995 The ATM Forum. See the Preface for further copyright
information.

Printed in the United States of America
10 9 8 7 6 5 4 3 2 1

ISBN 0-13-243700-7

Prentice-Hall International (UK) Limited, *London*
Prentice-Hall of Australia Pty. Limited, *Sydney*
Prentice-Hall Canada Inc., *Toronto*
Prentice-Hall Hispanoamericana, S.A., *Mexico*
Prentice-Hall of India Private Limited, *New Delhi*
Prentice-Hall of Japan, Inc., *Tokyo*
Simon & Schuster Asia Pte. Ltd., *Singapore*
Editora Prentice-Hall do Brasil, Ltda., *Rio de Janeiro*

Contents

Contents

List of Figures

List of Tables

Preface

MPEG-2 (digital video compression standard created by the Moving Pictures Experts Group) and ATM (Asynchronous Transfer Mode) can be regarded as the key technologies that will enable the digital video services to go past the academic stage and become a real end user success. These technologies are, however, only a small part of the Broadband Integrated Service Digital Network, or B-ISDN. When digital video services are distributed to the customers, the B-ISDN will be one of the most essential vehicles. Therefore, there will be a huge interaction and dependency between video services and the underlying network.

MPEG-2-based digital video will be one of the most important services in the emerging ATM-based B-ISDN network. It can be used to realize various different kinds of multimedia services such as video conferencing, video on demand, and video e-mail, to mention only a few. The huge amount of data that is to be transported in order to include video into the networks will however require new technologies, both in the video and the networking environment. Digital video is more than just another kind of data which is transported on the network. It introduces new aspects to the communication world, both in terms of requirements and problems. Digital video in broadband networks goes beyond the PC-based multimedia applications one can buy for todays home PCs. It is a complex world of data communication, telecommunication, video technology, and terminology.

The worlds of tele/data communication and video distribution have, until now, been quite separate. However, digital video has formed a link that will cause these two areas to eventually converge. Along with the present day transmission of voice and data, it is possible to transmit video and various interactive multimedia services on the existing tele/data communication networks, in a cost efficient manner. At the same time it is possible to use the infrastructure, which now serves only for the purpose of distributing TV and video, in order to convey, for instance, data and voice communication, hereby enabling telephone service and World Wide Web access.

The convergence of these two worlds promises a range of new opportunities for participants. At the same time it also demands knowledge of the various technologies involved. Most people working in the tele/data communication area will find that they need to understand a whole new set of terms and concepts when starting to work with digital video. Likewise, people working with television and video transmission will now need to know and understand not just digital video, but also the concepts and details of one of the most important networks that will carry video in the future—the B-ISDN.

This book explains not only the MPEG specifications and the ATM-based B-ISDN, it also covers the integration of these technologies, along with the work that is beeing done to transport digital video over the internet. Furthermore, in order to facilitate understanding of the video and audio compression technologies dealt with, an introduction to the basics of video and audio, along with the human sense of seeing and hearing, is given.

To get an overview of the main chapters, please refer to the so called "chapter on a page." This is placed on the first page of each of the main chapters and introduces the basic content, along with the preferred context the chapter should be seen in. An explanation of the acronyms used is found at the end of the book. Finally, to probe further, please refer to the list of references.

Acknowledgments

The authors would like to thank the people of IDACOM, as well as Pat Pekary of Hewlett-Packard press and Karen Gettman of Prentice Hall, for their excellent support. A very special thanks to Tine Kristensen for excellent guidance and assistance throughout the creation of this book.

Please note that this book, by no means, can replace the relevant standards. It is meant as an introduction, which will provide a sufficient level of detail for some people and merely a starting point for others. Also, it is focused on what is perceived as the central areas by the authors, so some areas are dealt with sporadically, or completely ignored. For those who need to know the subject in more than an introductory level, we recommend study of the specific (standard) documents in detail. The specific documents can be found in the list of references.

Specifically, a number of the illustrations in the section of this book that describes MPEG is based on illustrations found in the standards ISO/IEC 11172-1/2/3 and 13818-1/2/3/6. This is done with the permission of the International Standard for Standardization (ISO) and International Electrotechnical Commission (IEC). These standards can be obtained from any ISO member or from the ISO Central Secretariat. The copyright remains with ISO and IEC.

Furthermore, a number of the illustrations in the book are based on illustrations found in International Telecommunication Union (ITU) recommendations, as well as the relevant standards, as seen in the list of references. This is done with the prior authorization of the ITU as copyright holder. The responsibility for selecting the illustrations lies with the authors and can in no way be attributed to the ITU.

Please refer to Appendix A for the addresses of the ITU and ISO, as well as other organizations relevant for the subjects dealt with.

1

Introduction

1.1 New Services and New Technologies

The term "multimedia" has lately become one of the most over-used words in the information processing industry. Different interpretations can be found for what multimedia actually means, but generally speaking, it is a way to present information by combining still pictures, text, audio, and video. Multimedia applications can be implemented on a stand-alone computer, like a PC, or they can be implemented in a distributed system based on some kind of digital network. If user control is implemented, the multimedia application becomes "interactive."

Interactivity is not something new in computer environments, where text and graphics have been used to feed information back and forth to and from users for a long time. Some of the newer building blocks for multimedia do, however, require a certain level of system and equipment performance. This performance was only recently achieved. One of the most performance demanding aspects of multimedia is undoubtedly video.

Of course, video itself is nothing completely new. The most important video application we know today is TV broadcasting, and it is based on analog technology. Digital video, however, was until some time ago only used in the studio and production arena. Some recent developments, both in data compression techniques and network technologies, will make it possible to use digital video in other application environments.

One example is to use video in data networks. The recent explosive growth of the Internet and World Wide Web applications have caused interest in integrating digital video into the Internet environment. There is, of course, an easy way to accomplish this by downloading a file with video data to a user's PC and then starting playback. This makes sense for very short video clips, where download time might be acceptable. To watch a whole movie, there is currently no way to get around the so called streamed video. In this case, video pictures are sent continuously ("streamed") from a central server to a client, where they are decoded and displayed as soon as they arrive.

However, there are some issues in streaming video with data network protocols. One is the fact that streaming digital video data demands a set of very specific requirements from the network. Digital video data streams are very sensitive to delays and transmission errors, which can be caused by data networks for different reasons. Also, streaming digital video data usually means transporting one to three Megabits per second to the consumer, which is beyond the bandwidth capabilities, which the residential access network technologies for data services currently support. The Internet community, namely the Internet Engineering Task Force (IETF), is trying to address these issues. We will briefly cover the subject of video in the Internet in Chapter 6.

Parallel to the efforts of resolving issues in delivering digital video via established data networks, the cable TV service operators and their technology suppliers try to enhance the already established TV cable networks with new services. The main challenge in enhancing pure video services (like cable TV, terrestrial broadcast TV, or satellite TV direct to the home) is the question of how to realize a two-way communication, or in other words, how to implement a path back from the consumer to the service provider in order to allow interactivity. Some very promising technologies, which might solve this problem, are currently showing up at the horizon. We will have a look at those technologies in Chapter 5 when we examine the different access networks. Interestingly enough, these technologies might also help to deliver digital video with the above mentioned data networks, like the Internet.

To summarize, new multimedia services can be realized by (at least) two different approaches, as illustrated in Fig. 1.1. The first approach is to start with data communication and data processing technology in order to implement interactive data services. Examples for these interactive data services are the World Wide Web, based on the Internet, and the commercial on-line services that are offered by various providers. These interactive data services were originally text-based but are now implemented with a graphical user interface. The next step in this development process is to include video into the services.

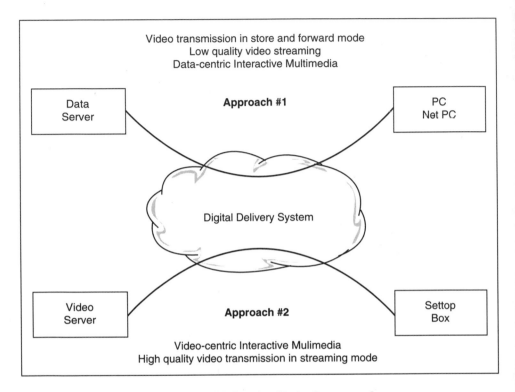

Figure 1.1: Video in digital networks

The second approach is to supplement the current television broadcast service with interactivity. Along with this goes the introduction of digital technology for delivery and storing of video and audio information. Once the interactive component has been added, new kinds of services can be built. The standard TV broadcasting then becomes part of a suite of services built around the key component—high quality digital video.

Both approaches have in common the fact that they use digital video to deliver information to the consumer, although the delivery is implemented in different ways.

By using digital technologies for information storage, manipulation, and transmission, we gain huge opportunities to create new kinds of services and to process information in new and flexible ways. The services that are implemented following the second approach, are highly focused on the use of video as a medium to deliver information. In this approach, the services are related to the television we are used to now, but they add new aspects, such as user control or two-way communication in general. Some examples of these new video based services are listed in Table 1.1.

If we look at the first approach, digital video is mainly used to enhance the presentation, exchange, and delivery of information. Please see Table 1.2 for applications that will use video as an additional information medium.

The new services and applications described above (especially the video-based services) have in common the fact that they require the delivery of huge amounts of data, typically 20-30 full-color pictures per second, to the consumer. In other words the content that is transmitted is getting very complex and requires a lot of bandwidth to be delivered to the user. However, the complex content is not the only reason why there is a need for more bandwidth in the networks. There are at least two other issues:

- The architecture of the applications using the network is getting more and more client-server oriented. This requires more and more communications, which are not visible to the user. Applications are going to be implemented by soft-

Service	Description
Movies on Demand (MoD)	A Movies on Demand (MoD) service will implement "VCR-like" functionality via a network. The consumer does not have to go to a video rental shop and get a video cassette. The movie will be delivered via the network. MoD can include features like fast forward, slow motion, start, stop, etc.
News on Demand	With News on Demand, the consumer will be able to create her own personalized news program. The news program could be customized in terms of the amount of video, text and audio information. Also, only news on specific topics could be selected and delivered.
Near Video on Demand (NVoD)	Near Video on Demand (NVoD) is broadcasting the same program on different channels, with different start times. The consumer chooses the channel where a program is about to start. To resume watching after a pause, the consumer chooses the channel that is a certain amount of time "behind" the channel he/she watched before. Near Video on Demand does not require a communication channel from the user to the service provider, which makes it relatively simple to implement.

Table 1.1: New video services.

Application	Description
Word Wide Web	Clicking on a symbol starts the transmission of video to the user's browser.
Personal Video Conferencing	The user is able to join a video conference by using a desktop computer.
Desktop Video-telephony	The common telephone service, but with visual contact to the other party.

Table 1.2: Desktop applications including video.

ware components, which are communicating with each other. This essential communication requires bandwidth.

- The number of clients and servers is rapidly growing. The network has to cope with an increasing number of participants, where each participant might use complex content and client-server oriented software applications.

This increasing need for bandwidth and processing power is valid for all the different parts of a video service delivery architecture. This architecture typically consists of the (video) server system, a core or transport network, the access network, and the consumer device. Fig. 1.2 shows these major components.

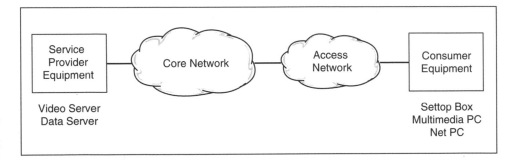

Figure 1.2: Service delivery architecture.

The industry is addressing the bandwidth requirement by developing new and faster network technologies and compression technologies for bandwidth consuming content.

The main focus of this book deals with network technologies, digital video technologies, and the way they fit together. However, we will focus only on those that are considered as internationally accepted standards and that are more or less finalized at the time of this writing. Also, we will not cover the use of digital video in the studio environment, consumer entertainment devices, or any proprietary digital video or network technologies.

1.1.1 Network Technologies: Broadband ISDN and ATM

In 1988, the Asynchronous Transfer Mode (ATM) was defined by the International Telecommunication Union (ITU) as a vehicle for the future Broadband ISDN (B-ISDN). B-ISDN is intended to become the universal network to transport all kinds of service data, including video. The ITU-T B-ISDN recommendations foresees some video-related services:

- Broadband video-telephony
- Broadband video conferencing
- Video-surveillance
- Video mail
- Video retrieval
- Existing quality TV distribution (PAL, SECAM, NTSC)
- High Definition TV distribution
- Pay-TV

The ATM technology that was chosen for the B-ISDN promised to be flexible and fast enough to support all the requirements demanded by these new services. ATM is expected to be used in the core network. The core network is the central transmission system between the service providers and the access networks, which together connect the consumer. The use of ATM is, however, not restricted to the core network; it can also be used in the access network. Eventually, it might be used all the way to an end user device, like a desktop computer or a set top box.

However, even with ATM, the amount of data generated by uncompressed video services is still hard to handle. To represent only one second of raw uncompressed video data (using broadcast quality), around 270 million bits are required. The bandwidth and hardware resources that would be needed to transmit this amount of data would make the service much too expensive. This triggered a number of research activities with the goal to reduce the amount of data that has to be transmitted. A widely accepted solution was found by compressing the video and audio data according to Moving Pictures Experts Group (MPEG) standards.

1.1.2 Digital Video Technologies: ISO/IEC's Moving Pictures Experts Group (MPEG)

In 1988, the ISO/IEC established the Moving Pictures Experts Group (MPEG) in order to define a standard for video and audio compression. The group developed the MPEG-1 standard, which is today mainly used in CD-ROM video applications. However, MPEG-1 is not suited for broadcast environments or television applications, as it does not support all the features required for these applications. Therefore, ISO/IEC started to work on the MPEG-2 standard in 1990. The work on the major parts of MPEG-2 was finished in late 1994, so that MPEG-2 equipment is already available.

Digital video will bring totally new applications, both in the area of TV, interactive information systems, and entertainment systems. MPEG-2, as an example, will also be used with new storage media like the Digital Versatile Disk (DVD). DVD will bring MPEG-2 to PCs and consumer DVD players. However, MPEG-2 is not the end of the story and ISO/IEC is moving forward to produce common standards for new applications of digital video. MPEG-3 was intended to address high-definition TV applications, but it turned out that MPEG-2 could cover this functionality. As a consequence, no MPEG-3 standard was made. Currently, ISO/IEC is working on the MPEG-4 suite of standards. One of the objectives here is to make it possible to mix and combine virtual images (like computer animations) and real video images on a bitstream level. Applications for this can be games, video mail, helper agents, etc.

1.1.3 Network Technologies: Access Networks

Delivering digital video to the consumer requires access to the home with a high bit rate media. For acceptable quality, MPEG-2 compressed video and a bit rate of at least 3 MBit/s is required. New technologies in the access networks must be in place to allow this high bit rate transmission to the consumer. A big challenge in this context is avoiding digging up the last mile to the home in order to deploy a new transmission media. Therefore, several technologies have been invented to make use of the existing cables that are already installed to our homes. In regions where cable TV is deployed, the existing cable infrastructure can be used to deliver new services. For other regions, new technologies like Asymmetric Digital Subscriber Line (ADSL) can exploit the existing telephone network in order to deliver high bit rates.

However, if there is a need to deploy new cables in a residential area, fiber is installed up to a central point. The existing coax cable network can then be connected with the fiber. Concepts that follow this approach are Fiber To The Curb (FTTC), Fiber To The Building (FTTB), and Hybrid Fiber-Coax (HFC). The method giving the highest performance in terms of transmission speed is provided by terminating the fiber at the consumer premise. This approach is also known as Fiber To The Home (FTTH) technology.

11

Beside these technologies, which are all based on cable networks, wireless access networks using microwave transmission have been developed. Examples of these wireless technologies are Local (LMDS) or Multichannel Multipoint Distribution System (MMDS).

1.1.4 Video in Future Information Systems

Even with a high speed network available for connection, new kinds of end user equipment have to be developed to access the mentioned services in Table 1.1 and 1.2. On the service provider side, the equipment has to store large amounts of data (several terabytes for a video library) and deliver this data to the network. Video servers, or more generally named, "media servers," with huge storage capability and I/O performance were recently developed by major computer vendors.

On the consumer side, PCs with multimedia and network extensions can be used if the multimedia services are based on interactive data technology. MPEG-2 decoders for PCs and workstations are available in hardware and software implementations. Set-top units or cable modems connecting a TV set or a PC to different access network technologies are currently developed by major consumer electronic and computer companies.

Beside these new pieces of hardware, a major change in the information processing software is taking place.

The World Wide Web technology, which we see being used today in the public and private Internets, is actually only the beginning of a new wave of client-server, or distributed, computing. Client-server systems are, of course, not a totally new concept. However, a major breakthrough was achieved some time ago with the definition of two widely accepted distributed computing software architectures: The *Common Request Broker Architecture (CORBA)* and the *Object Linking and Embedding / Distributed Component Object Model (OLE / DCOM)*. Both are basically a communication platform (sometimes also called *software bus*), which is used by software components to communicate with each other. It can be compared with the bus system in a PC, which is used to connect different hardware components. The Web protocols and standards help on the consumer side to make it easy to access information and to interface with the systems providing information. The software buses help on the server side to build information systems offering all kind of services. Even if we are in a quite early stage with the implementation of software bus systems, it is regarded as one of the major developments helping us to build flexible and powerful information systems.

Digital video will be one of the information types that will be used by these information systems and that will be implemented with the help of software components. A first approach to make digital video ready to fit into future information systems is done with the MPEG-2 DSM-CC user-to-user standard, which is using CORBA to define interfaces to the outside world. We will have a closer look on DSM-CC user-to-user standards in Chapter 3.

If we look at all of these emerging components of multimedia information systems (e.g., MPEG, ATM, set-top units, media servers, software technologies, access network technologies, and Internet technology), it becomes obvious that some effort is required to get a common understanding of how the building blocks should work together. Different approaches are undertaken in this area, with the one driven by the

Digital Audio Visual Council (DAVIC) as one of the most important. DAVIC's goal is to develop an overall reference model for multimedia systems. This includes a description of the different components belonging to the system, the creation of well defined interfaces between those components, and specifications of the formats of data that are exchanged at these interfaces. We will cover the network related aspects of the DAVIC model in Chapter 6.

2

Video and Audio Fundamentals

2.1 Video and Audio Fundamentals—On a Page

To enable better understanding of the sections of this book that deal with the MPEG video and audio compression, this chapter will give an introduction to some central aspect of the human sense of seeing and hearing. Furthermore, the basic terms and concepts of digital processing, and representation of video and audio information will be dealt with. The chapter will cover:

- Video fundamentals: This section will first focus on a few central aspects of the human sense of seeing. This is followed by an introduction to colorspaces, including representation forms of pictures (RGB and YUV), as well as sampling. Finally the aspects of interlacing and specific digital video formats are covered (ITU-R 601, SIF and CIF).

- Audio fundamentals: This section will first focus on a few central aspects of the human sense of hearing, including some of the characteristics utilized in the compression algorithms (like the masking effect for instance). This is followed by a brief introduction to time and frequency domain representation of signals, as well as concepts such as SNR. Finally the basic principles of A/D and D/A conversion of audio signals are described.

2.2 Video Fundamentals

2.2.1 Aspects of the Human Sense of Seeing

A major goal of the MPEG-2 video standard is to define the format of the video data to be transmitted. This data format is the result of a compression and encoding process. Compression techniques, which are used in MPEG-2, are to a large extent based on the knowledge we have about how the human eye and the visual centers in the brain recognize images.

During the process of seeing, the eye has to fulfill two main tasks. First, the eye has to recognize details of a scene, which means it has to perceive the spatial resolution of the picture. The second task is to recognize changes in a scene, in other words, to perceive a temporal resolution of a scene.

The term "seeing," as such, actually only describes the idea that light reflected by the objects surrounding us enters our eyes. The eye itself contains several parts that process reflected light and generate the image that our brain understands. When light has entered our eye, it passes through the cornea, the iris, the pupil and finally the lens. All these parts work together to put a focused image onto the back of the eye, which is called the retina. Once on the retina, the image can be recognized and processed by the brain. To process the image information in the brain, the retina is equipped with photoreceptors, which are stimulated differently.

There are two different kinds of photoreceptors: rods and cones. (These names are based on their actual shapes). It was found that with the rods, we are able to see black and white; while the cones give us the ability to distinguish between different colors. There are different kind of cones, which are especially sensitive for red, green and blue color. If light is reflected on a high number of cones, the cones then enable us to get a high spatial resolution of the image since small changes in the color can be recognized. Rods are more sensitive to the intensity of light itself. An important aspect of the rods and cones in the context of digital video is their number and their distribution on the retina. If we look for an example on the center of the retina we will only find cones. Areas further away from the center have a much higher distribution of rods. This is the reason why we have to look directly at some image to get all the details. This can be illustrated by a small experiment:

Place one hand on the page opposite this page and stay focused on this sentence. You are hardly able to recognize details on your hand, such as the texture of the skin. Please note that the distance to your hand is not much different from the distance to the print on this page, which means that it is not the lens that is causing the lack of detail. Only if you look directly at your hand (and by doing this, get the image in the center of the retina) will the level of detail improve.

In total, we have about one hundred and twenty million rods and only around eight million cones on the retina. The latter, as stated, are distributed close to the center of the retina. This leads to the fact that the eye is, in general, relatively less sensitive to color, especially to color changes. Video compression techniques, like the one used in MPEG-2 Video, therefore utilize this low-color sensitivity by reducing the color information per image. MPEG-2 uses Discrete Cosine Transformation (DCT) to identify and subsequently remove high frequency changes in color.

2.2.2 Colorspaces

So far, the human eye and its capabilities to recognize images have been described. But how are the images described and structured in digital equipment? Video applications deal with so called color spaces in order to define images. A color space is basically a theoretical model describing how to separate a color into different components. It also defines the meaning of these components. There are two major types of color spaces used in digital video: RGB and YUV/YCrCb. RGB is commonly used in computer environments, while YUV/YCrCb is related more to the television world.

RGB (Red, Green, Blue)

In the RGB color spaces, each pixel on the screen has a corresponding RGB value. The RGB value is built out of three components, which define a value for the red, the green and the blue parts of the color. Equal parts of red, green, and blue added together will result in white, grey, or black.

In computer environment, a number of bits are assigned for each pixel to carry color information. To be able to reproduce all the colors a human eye can see in the real world, it was found that each component of RGB must be described by 8 bits. This results in 2^{24} (16,777,216) different colors that can be represented.

However, the RGB color spaces have some disadvantages. One problem is the fact that the same amount of bits are needed for each of its components in order to create all possible colors. Also, RGB is not so well suited for television applications. If one would like to increase the brightness of a TV image with "RGB remote control," this would mean that it would be necessary to increase the value for each of the RGB components equally. In the television world, another color space is used, which is *YUV* and the related *YCrCb*.

YUV and YCrCb

YUV separates color information differently than RGB. Instead of breaking the color down to red, green, and blue components, it is split into intensity (Y) and two color components (U and V). The Y component, which is basically black and white information, is also called *luminance*. The U and V components are called *chrominance*.

For TV applications, this color space has some important advantages. First of all, it is easy to support black and white displays as well as color displays with this color space. A black and white display only uses the luminance component of the signal, the color display will use both luminance and chrominance information. YUV also fits better with our perception of color, as we are used to dealing with brightness and color. Finally, the YUV color space actually follows the processing structure of the human eye by differentiating the visual information into two parts (see Section 2.2.2). The video compression technique, used in MPEG-1 and MPEG-2 works with YUV color space.[1] Related to YUV, there is YCrCb, which is defined by the ITU-R 601 recommendation. Again, the Y, Cr, and Cb values can be generated out of RGB by applying some simple multiplications and additions.

---

[1]The YUV and the RGB color spaces are related to each other in terms of some simple formulas. The Y value for instance can be calculated by using the following equation:

$$Y = 0.299*R+0.587*G+0.114*B.$$

For U and V there are similar formulas.

2.2.3 Sampling of Chrominance and Luminance Values

In digital video, for each pixel there is color information in the form of color component values (e.g., for Y, Cr, Cb), which are defined. However, for some applications, like TV broadcasting, the color information for each pixel can be less accurate than the luminance information. In this case, it is possible to assign color information, for example, only to every second pixel. This method is described by the "colon notation," as for instance, 4:2:2. This notation basically describes the relation between the number of luminance and chrominance samples taken while digitizing video pictures:

- 4:4:4 Sampling Ratio: In this case, luminance (intensity) and chrominance (color) information and are present for every pixel. Fig. 2.1 shows rows of pixels with Y, Cr, and Cb information assigned for each pixel.

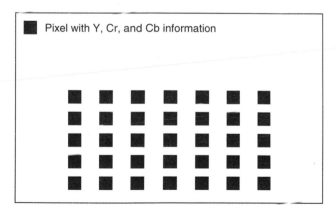

Figure 2.1: Y, Cr, and Cb distribution for 4:4:4.

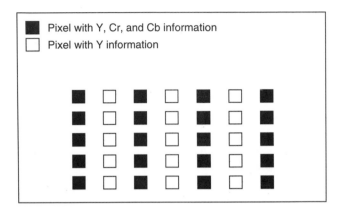

Figure 2.2: Y, Cr, and Cb distribution for 4:2:2.

- 4:2:2 Sampling Ratio: In this case, luminance (intensity) is present for every pixel and chrominance (color) information is present for every second pixel in the horizontal direction. This example is shown in Fig. 2.2.

- 4:2:0 and 4:1:1 Sampling Ratio: The 4:2:0 and the 4:1:1, formats further reduce the number of chrominance samples. For 4:2:0 and 4:1:1 chrominance information is only available for every fourth pixel. The 4:2:0 format is a special case of 4:1:1, where the chrominance values are calculated and therefore represent a value that is offset from luminance samples (see Fig. 2.3).

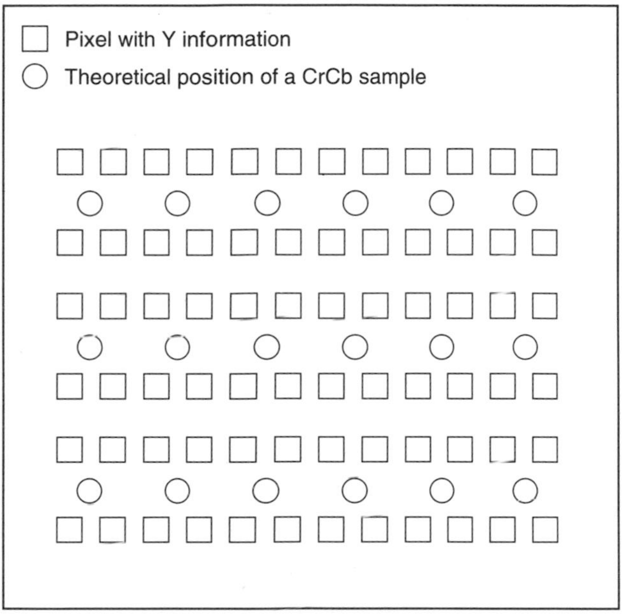

Figure 2.3: Y, Cr, and Cb distribution for 4:2:0.

2.2.4 Interlacing

Another essential term in the context of digital video is interlacing. Interlacing is a technique that is used in TV and computer display applications. Computer displays and TV sets are based on the Cathode Ray Tube (CRT) technology, where an electron beam is used to create a picture. The beam is projected against the TV screen, which on the inner side is covered with phosphor particles. Where the beam hits the phosphor particles, a dot will light up for a short period of time.

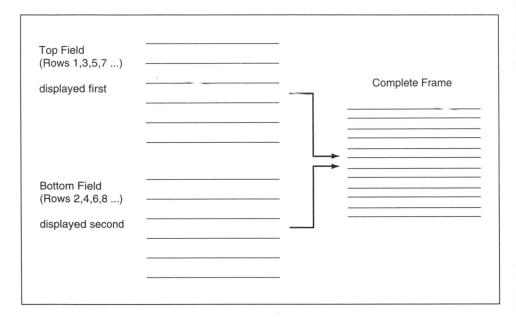

Figure 2.4: Two fields forming a frame.

But even though the electron beam is moved very quickly across the screen, the top lines are already fading away at the point in time where the beam reaches the bottom line. This fading of the image would be recognized by the human eye as a flickering of the image. To avoid this effect, interlacing is used. Interlacing basically splits one image (the frame,) which has to be displayed, into two images (the fields), which contain half of the information of the original image. Fig. 2.4 shows this concept. The first field consists only of the odd horizontal lines of the frame, the even horizontal lines belong to the second field. Both fields are projected into the CRT, one after another. However, when the first field starts to fade away, the second field has already been projected by the beam, showing nearly the same information. As a result, the eye will not get the impression of a flicker. Also, the beam only needs half the time to project a field and can then return to the top to project the next field.

2.2.5 Digital Video Formats

If video is represented digitally, there are quite a few options regarding the horizontal and vertical resolution of the picture, the number of pictures per second, and the number of bits used to store the color information. If different applications should handle digital video material, it is necessary that all of these applications have a common understanding of the above mentioned parameters. The most important digital video formats are therefore described below.

ITU-R 601 Recommendation

The ITU-R recommendation 601 (also known more commonly under its old name, CCIR-601) defines the basic parameters for digitizing analog video material. It therefore covers both major TV standards, PAL with 625 lines per frame and 25 frames per second, as well as NTSC with 525 lines per frame and 30 frames per second. For the described 4:2:2 sampling ratio (see Section 2.2.4), a picture encoded according to ITU-R 601 has 858 (NTSC) or 864 (PAL) samples per line for the luminance (Y) component and 429 (NTSC) or 432 (PAL) samples per line for both chrominance (Cr and Cb) components.

A picture encoded with the 4:4:4 ratio provides 858 (NTSC) or 864 (PAL) samples for all components (Y, Cr, and Cb). However, some of the

sample ratio	samples per digital active line for Y component	samples per digital active line for Cr component	samples per digital active line for Cb component	bits needed per second (8 bits per component, 25 frames/sec and 625 lines)
4:4:4	720	720	720	270 Mbit
4:2:2	720	360	360	180 Mbit

Table 2.1: ITU-R 601 parameters.

samples are taken during the blanking period, where the electron beam is not actually projecting an image. Therefore, the number of digital active samples and lines is smaller. Table 2.1 summarizes the digital active lines and samples as defined by ITU-R 601.

Beside the sampling ratio, ITU-R 601 also defines the YCrCb color-space by describing the different formulas to derive the YCrCb values from the values of RGB.

Source Input Format (SIF) and Common Interchange Format (CIF)

The Source Input Format (SIF) and Common Interchange Format (CIF) are digital video formats that are defined by the MPEG-1 and the ITU-T H.261 Video Conferencing Recommendation. The SIF format specifies the luminance resolution of a frame to be 360 x 242 pixels for 30 frames/per second systems. For 25 frames/per second systems, SIF

Horizontal/ Vertical Resolutions	SIF (30 frames per second)	SIF (25 frames per second)	CIF (30 frames per second)
Y	360 x 242	360 x 288	352 x 288
Cr	180 x 121	180 x 144	176 x 144
Cb	180 x 121	180 x 144	176 x 144
Sampling Format	4:2:0	4:2:0	4:2:0

Table 2.2: SIF and CIF parameters.

defines a luminance resolution of 360 x 288 pixels. The sampling format for SIF is 4:2:0.

The CIF format was developed in the context of the ITU-T H.261 recommendation in order to have a common format to which PAL- and NTSC-based frames could be converted. CIF uses a frame rate of 30 frames per second and a resolution of 352 x 288 pixels for the luminance component. The sampling format in CIF is also 4:2:0. Table 2.2 summarizes the parameters for SIF and CIF.

2.3 Audio fundamentals

2.3.1 Aspects of the Human Sense of Hearing

Human hearing is quite a complex mechanism, to say the least. We hear with our ears, obviously—but that is actually only the starting point. Our ears turn sound—alternating air pressure—into signals that are to be "processed" and interpreted by our brain. Our hearing system consists of many subsystems, of which only a few of the most relevant are touched upon here.

When we hear a sound, the sound is first turned into mechanical impulses by a membrane connected to three small bones in the inner ear. The tympanic membrane, as it is called, and the three small bones—the hammer, anvil, and stirrup—lead the vibrations to a spiral shaped liquid filled organ called the cochlea. The cochlea contains many very fine hairs, which are connected to nerves leading to the hearing center in the brain. (Small hairs in different locations [depth] of the cochlea are stimulated at different frequencies.) The actual perception and understanding of the audible information takes place in the hearing center.

An interesting phenomenon of the human sense of hearing is masking: When a loud tone at a specific frequency stimulates the hairs of the cochlea, the frequencies close to the first powerful tone are not heard if they are less powerful. This is also called the "masking effect." Fig. 2.5 is a model of this. Say, there is a powerful frequency at 1.2 KHz. Even though there are many other frequencies present and close to this dominant tone, it masks them, and our hearing does not perceive, for instance, the tone at 1.1 KHz, which is 18 dB weaker. The powerful 1.2 KHz tone cannot, however, mask the tone at 2 KHz, which is also

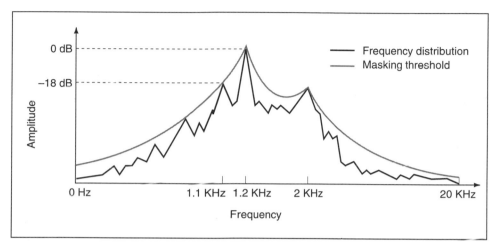

Figure 2.5: Masking effect with dominating 1.2 KHz frequency.

18 dB lower, as it is relatively far from the 1.2 KHz tone. The 2 KHz tone also has a masking effect on nearby frequencies. Masking from the 1.2 and the 2 KHz tones are added, so that a fair curve stretches between the frequencies, masking everything lying below it (i.e., we hear nothing).

2.3.2 Basic Terms and Concepts

- Frequency sensitivity: Our hearing is not equally sensitive to all frequencies. We are most sensitive to frequencies in the range from 1 to 3 KHz. It is not surprising that in this frequency range we find most of the sounds of "interest" to us, such as voices.

- Directivety: We also tend to be most sensitive to the directivety of sounds, in the frequency range of 0.2—3 KHz. This means it is virtually impossibly for us to say where a frequency at, for instance, 100 Hz comes from. It may be from the left, it may be from the right—we can't tell. This effect is to some extent experienced with tones at high frequencies, as well. It can, for instance, be very difficult to localize a tone at 10 KHz.

- Temporal masking: Our hearing is not only masking frequencies that fall close to a powerful frequency, as explained above. There is also a masking effect over time at powerful transients (a shift in 30—40 dB). If one hears the shot of a gun for instance, it is not possible to hear anything just after the shot. Interestingly enough, it is also not possible to hear anything just before. This is called pre- and post-masking. Pre-masking is of a short duration, 2–5 ms; post-masking can last up to 100 ms. In this period of time, very little other than the transient that causes the masking will be perceived.

These psychoacoustic properties of our hearing system are actually the starting point where efficient compression algorithms are made. There are, as seen above, a lot of auditory information that reaches our ear, but much of it we will never perceive anyway, due to, among other things, the masking effect. Therefore, the compression methods used in MPEG-1 and MPEG-2 remove a lot of the redundant information in order to achieve their compression rates.

What is sound then? Sound is simply a propagation of alternating air pressures, which in free space spreads like rings in all three dimensions. It is a change of momentum from one air molecule to the next.

When sound travels through air, it does so at a speed of approximately 342 m/s (at 20° C). When somebody, for instance, blows a whistle, he makes waves of air with higher, respectively lower air pressure which emanate from the whistle with a certain frequency. The frequency range humans can hear is normally considered to be in the range of 16–20,000 Hz. Sound with a frequency below 16 Hz cannot be heard, but one can feel it if it is powerful enough. Frequencies above 20,000 Hz cannot be registered by any of the human senses.

When representing sound there are two common ways. One is to represent the amplitude of the signal as it changes over time. This is called the "time domain" (amplitude versus time). The second method is to represent the amplitude of the different frequencies at a given moment. This is called the "frequency domain" (amplitude versus frequency). See Fig. 2.6.

Which domain one selects as appropriate depends on what aspects of the signal one wishes to observe. If the exact power of different specific frequencies is of interest, or if one wishes to get just a general overview of the frequency distribution of a given signal, the frequency domain is chosen. The drawback is that one cannot get any detailed information of waveshape or other time domain related information out of the frequency domain representation. The time domain representation is chosen if one has specific interests in the waveshape. This could include interests in various indications of distortion, as well as parameters (signal symmetry, rise and fall time, peak, average or RMS[2] amplitude of the signal, etc.)

There are several ways of measuring the level (amplitude) of sound. One of the most common is to measure in decibel Sound Pressure Level, or dB SPL. Decibel is a logarithmic expression of a given level, compared with a certain reference level. When a sound level is repre-

---

[2]RMS = Root Mean Square

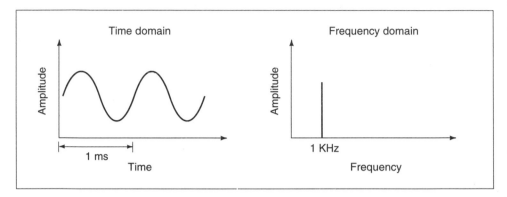

Figure 2.6: Time and frequency
domain representation of the same signal.

sented in dB SPL, it simply means that the sound pressure (or rather an average value over time) is represented in decibels, referring to a reference pressure of 20 micro Pascal. The reason why the amplitude of sound is normally represented in decibels, is that this type of scale allows one to represent a very wide range in a manageable space. If one wishes to represent amplitudes from 0 to 120 dB, it would be equivalent to a factor 1,000,000 on a linear scale. This would be quite impractical, as details of the signal would disappear completely. As sounds of the magnitude 120 dB are not uncommon (at concerts for instance), this also indicates that our sense of hearing covers a wide amplitude range. In other words, we can hear sounds with an immense difference in magnitude.

In connection with the reproduction of sound, one often meets the Signal to Noise Ratio, or SNR. In virtually all systems that reproduce sound (microphone, amplifier, digitalization, etc.), noise is introduced to the original signal. The amplitude of this noise may vary among dif-

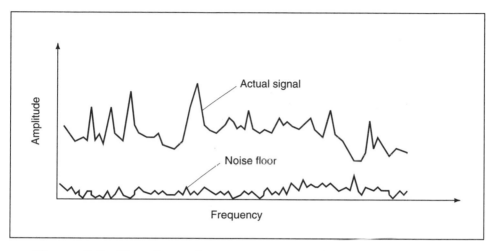

Figure 2.7: Signal to noise ratio—actual signal and noise floor.

ferent system types. A classic example is that the noise on CDs is lower than that on traditional vinyl recordings. Signal to noise ratio is simply the difference in magnitude (amplitude) between the actual signal (music, speech, etc.) and the noise introduced by the system. (See Fig. 2.7.) For CDs, this difference is typically about 90 dB. (So the "noise floor" is 90 dB weaker than the signal.) The noise floor is normally only heard in quiet passages where the actual signal is too weak to "cover" the noise, if it is heard at all.

2.3.3 Digital Representation of Sound

Sound can be stored and manipulated digitally, as seen with CDs. The process of storing sound digitally generally involves three steps:

1. The pressure differences in air is converted by the microphone to a corresponding alternating voltage level.

2. The voltage level is amplified to a suitable level and filters cut off frequencies, which are out of the range the A/D converter can handle.

3. The A/D converter samples the alternating voltage level a specified number of times per second (sample frequency, or fs) and converts it to a binary code with a certain number of bits (resolution). In other words, the signal is "quantized." (See Fig. 2.8.)

The third step is the one with the highest relevance for this introduction. In CD quality audio, the incoming alternating voltage level is sampled by the A/D converter 44.100 times per seconds. Each sample is converted to a 16 bit value. The practical outcome of CD audio is the ability to represent from 0-20.000 Hz, with a maximum theoretical dynamic range of approximately 96 dB due to the 16 bit resolution.[3]

Many other combinations of sampling rate and resolution can be used:

- The constraints for the sample rate lies in how high the frequencies are that one wishes to represent. It is necessary to have a minimum number of samples of a certain waveform in order to be able to recreate it. To be specific, in theory, the very minimum is two samples per period. This was defined as early as 1924 by the Nyquist Theorem that says in order to represent one period, one must have

---

[3]The following describes the relationship between the resolution in bits, and the corresponding theoretical dynamic range. ("N" is number of bits):

$$Dynamic\_Range = 20LOG(2^N)$$

Example: 16 bits resolution => 20 LOG 2^{16} = 96.33 dB

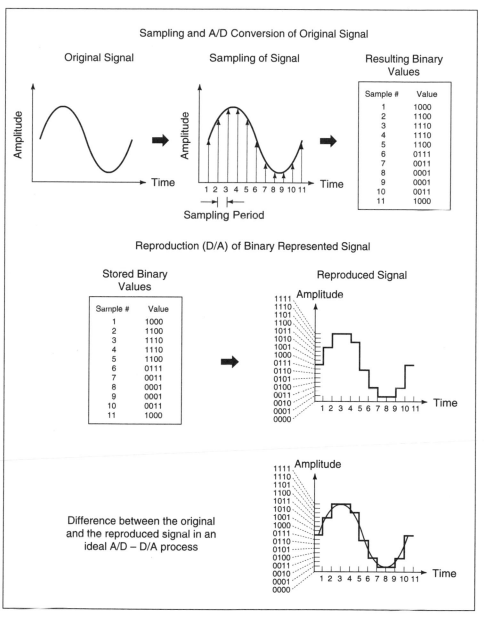

Figure 2.8: A/D and D/A conversion,(4 bits resolution) along with the resulting quantisation error.

no less than two samples of it. With less than two samples it is not possible to reconstruct the waveshape; this is valid, no matter what the frequency is. In reality, slightly more than two samples per period are used as a minimum.

The constraints of resolution are that of accuracy and noise. The higher the resolution (the more bits one uses to describe the value of each sample), the more precise one can describe a given amplitude and the lower the noise introduced from the A/D–D/A process will be. (The very small difference may be between the actual amplitude of the signal and the quantized value, which is also considered as noise. In an ideal A/D, this error value will be between 0 and $1/2$ LSB—in real life, it is normally more.)

2.4 To Get More Details . . .

The basic functions of the human eye and ear are normally described quite well in any encyclopedia. A discussion of different aspects of the human visual perception is given by the SMPTE [42]. To get more details about the digital video formats, ITU-R recommendations [23] and MPEG-1 video standards [35] have to be considered. To learn more about video in general, but always with the eyes of a digital engineer, Keith Jack's book [54] is a very good reference. For more detailed information on different topics relating to the human sense of hearing and audio processing in general, publications from the Audio Engineering Society, for instance [8], are recommended.

3

MPEG-2

3.1 MPEG-2—On a Page

The MPEG-2 standards outline the compression technologies and bit-stream syntax that enable transmission of audio and video in broad-band networks, which are found both in the broadcasting and telecommunications world. These standards also describe the aspects needed to multiplex programs, enable clock synchronization, as well as setup and use logical network links carrying video and audio content.

- Video Part: This section will first deal with the hierarchy of the objects used in an MPEG-2 compressed digital video (sequences, Group of Pictures, pictures, slices, macroblocks, and blocks). The actual compression methods as well as the resulting bit syntax, are then dealt with in detail, followed by a description of the scalability found in the standard.

- Audio Part: This section will first deal with the layered approach found in MPEG audio coding (layer 1, 2, and 3). This section then focuses specifically on the compression methods used in both MPEG-1 and MPEG-2, as well as the resulting bit syntax. Finally, the specific extensions of the MPEG-2 Audio compression, along with the aspects of backwards compatibility of MPEG-2 Audio, will be dealt with.

- Systems Part: This section will examine the functionality of the MPEG-2 Systems layer, especially the MPEG-2 transport streams. The main components of the transport stream will be explained, including elementary streams, packetized elementary streams, and program specific information. The section concludes with an overview about the time synchronization functionality of MPEG-2 transport streams.

- Digital Storage Media—Command and Control (DSM-CC) Part: This section will first deal with the structure of DSM-CC, followed by an detailed description of the DSM-CC user-to-network functionality. The section concludes with an overview about the DSM-CC user-to-user functionality.

3.2 The MPEG-2 Standards

MPEG-2 is, in many cases, associated only with video compression, which is certainly one of the most important parts of its functionality. However, the MPEG-2 family of standards includes more than just pure video subject. In total, there are eight different parts of the MPEG-2, covering the different aspects of digital video and audio delivery and representation. Table 3.1 shows the different MPEG-2 parts. In the following sections we will focus on the four most essential parts of MPEG-2, namely Video, Audio, Systems, and DSM-CC.

MPEG-2	Description
ISO/IEC 13818-1	Systems
ISO/IEC 13818-2	Video
ISO/IEC 13818-3	Audio
ISO/IEC 13818-4	Compliance
ISO/IEC 13818-5	Software Simulation
ISO/IEC 13818-6	Digital Storage Media—Command and Control (DSM-CC)
ISO/IEC 13818-9	Real-time Interface for System Decoders
ISO/IEC 13818-10	DSM Reference Script Format

Table 3.1: Parts of the MPEG-2 standard.

3.3 MPEG-2 Video

3.3.1 Introduction

The main goal of the MPEG-2 Video Part is to define a format that can be used to describe a coded video bitstream. This video bitstream is the output of an encoding process, which compresses the video picture information significantly. MPEG-2 does not specify the encoding method, it only defines the resulting bit stream. Furthermore, it defines how to decode this bit stream. At first glance, it might seem to be problematic that MPEG-2 does not specify the encoding process. However, it is exactly this that keeps the process open for enhancements, for instance reducing the encoding time or increasing picture quality.

When MPEG-2 was developed, one of the requirements was to make it flexible enough to handle a range of video applications. Some of those applications were:

- Broadcast (Satellite) Services
- Cable TV Distribution
- Interactive Television Services

Flexibility should result in the support of different video resolutions, equipment capabilities, network bandwidth constraints, and picture qualities. The MPEG-2 group managed to make the standard very generic by providing a set of tools that can be combined in different ways.

The MPEG-2 Video standard basically consists of the following parts:

- Basic definitions: Basic objects such as pictures and frames are defined.

- MPEG-2 Video syntax: Different syntax elements are defined in C-like pseudo-code.

- Semantic description for the video stream syntax: Semantic description is given for all syntax elements.

- Video decoding process: Video decoding processes are described, including decoding in interlaced and progressive mode.

- Scalability extensions: Different variants of scalability of MPEG-2 Video are described and the decoding for each mode is explained.

- Profiles and levels: Different profiles (set of features) and levels (set of values), which are used to define subsets of MPEG-2 Video, are described.

- Annexes: Annexes provide variable length coding tables, tables that define profile and level constraints, and the Discrete Cosine Transform (DCT) function. They also contain some informative sections.

This section will give an introduction to the terminology and the most important concepts of the video part of the MPEG-2 Standard.

3.3.2 MPEG-2 Video—The Basics

MPEG-2 deals with a number of basic objects that are used to structure video information. They are shown in Fig. 3.1.

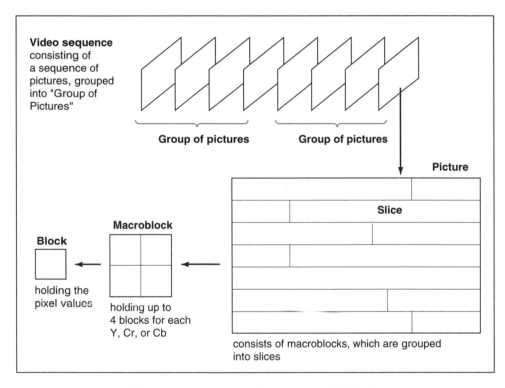

Figure 3.1: Basic objects in MPEG-2.

Video Sequence

The Video Sequence represents a number of video pictures or group of video pictures. Even if the name might give another impression, a video sequence contains only a few pictures and not a whole movie.

Frame

A frame contains all the color and brightness information that is needed to display a picture on the screen. The color and brightness information is organized into three matrices, which contain the luminance and chrominance values. The size of these matrices vary, depending on the supported resolution of the image and on the sampling ratio used. Fig. 3.2 show these matrices, for a 4:4:4 and a 4:2:2 sampled frame.

Pictures, Macroblocks, and Blocks

A picture is a very important object in MPEG-2 Video. Each picture is divided into a number of blocks, which are grouped into macroblocks. Each block contains eight lines, with each line holding eight samples of luminance or chrominance pixel values from a frame, as described in the previous section. This gives a total number of 64 chrominance or luminance pixel values defining a block.

Four blocks with luminance values, plus a number of blocks with chrominance values, form the luminance and chrominance information of a macroblock. The number of chrominance blocks in a macroblock depends on the sampling format used to digitize the video material:

45

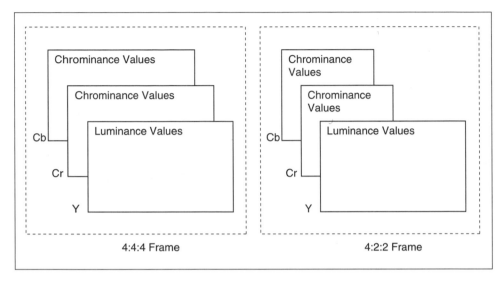

Figure 3.2: Matrices forming a 4:4:4 and a 4:2:2 frame.

- 4:2:0 macroblock: A 4:2:0 macroblock holds four blocks of luminance and two blocks of chrominance information.

- 4:2:2 macroblock: A 4:2:2 macro block holds four blocks of luminance and four blocks of chrominance information.

- 4:4:4 macroblock: A 4:4:4 macroblock holds four blocks with luminance and eight blocks of chrominance information.

Different macroblock formats are illustrated in Fig. 3.3. Each macroblock has a number that actually indicates the sequence in which the blocks of a macroblock are coded in MPEG-2 Video. As we can see the luminance values are always the first ones that are present in a

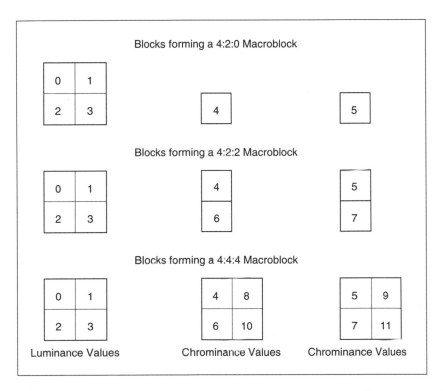

Figure 3.3: Macroblock formats of 4:4:4, 4:2:2 and 4:2:0.

macroblock. The interleaved blocks of Cb and Cr chrominance values then follow. By distributing the Cb and Cr values equally, some higher error robustness is achieved.

The described macroblocks are used to build the picture. There are three picture types defined in MPEG-2 Video:

- Intra-coded Pictures: Intra-coded pictures (*I-pictures*) are pictures that are coded in such a way that they can be decoded without knowing anything about other pictures in the video sequence. Because of this, in a video sequence or group of pictures, the first picture is always an I-picture and provides "bootstrap" information for the following pictures. I-pictures need the most bits to be represented, since all information of the picture is explicitly described in the bit stream. The blocks and macroblocks that are forming an I-picture are called *intra-blocks* or *intra-coded* macroblocks.

- Predictive Coded Pictures: Predictive coded pictures (*P-pictures*) are decoded by using information from another picture, which was displayed earlier (intercoding). This previous picture is also called *reference picture*, which could have been coded as an I-picture or as a P-picture. The information that can be used from the previous picture is determined by motion estimation (see section on data compression used in MPEG-2 Video) and is coded in what are called *inter-macroblocks* (I-macroblocks). Information that cannot be "borrowed" from reference pictures is coded in the same way I-pictures are coded. Because of this, a P-picture consists of intracoded macroblocks (*I-macroblocks*) and predictive coded macroblocks (*P-macroblocks*). The latter are always coming with a motion vector, indicating which macroblock to use from a previous picture. P-pictures are around 50-30 percent of the size of an I-picture.

- Bidirectionally Predicted Pictures: Bi-directionally coded pictures (*B-pictures*) also use information from other

48

pictures. Like P-pictures, they can use information provided by pictures that occurred before. Furthermore, B-pictures can also use information from a picture coming in the future. This is possible because at encoding time the encoder already has access to following pictures. As in P-pictures, picture information that cannot be found in previous or future pictures is intracoded. B-pictures are approximately 50 percent of the size of a P-picture.

Fig. 3.4 shows an example where it would make sense to encode a picture as a B-picture. The plane that is totally hidden by the cloud in picture #1 starts to appear in picture #2. If this picture would be coded as a B-picture, the clouds could be "borrowed" from picture #1 and the front part of the plane could be taken from picture #4. Picture #4 would be coded as a P-picture. It would use the clouds from picture #1 and only the plane would actually be coded in the P-picture.

The different pictures are distinguished by means of the MPEG-2 Video syntax. For each picture an indication is given if it is an I-, P-, or B-picture. Using the three picture types described above, a sequence of pictures can look like Fig. 3.5.

Fig. 3.5 shows that, if the decoder has to decode this sequence of pictures, it has to know about P-picture #4 in order to decode the B-pictures #2 and #3. Therefore, the pictures are not transmitted in the same order in which they will be displayed later on. A reordering takes place before the sequence is sent to the receiver. To display the sequence in the order shown in Fig. 3.5, the pictures would be transmitted in the order seen in Fig. 3.6.

Besides the picture reordering, B-pictures also require more memory in the decoder because an additional frame needs to be stored for

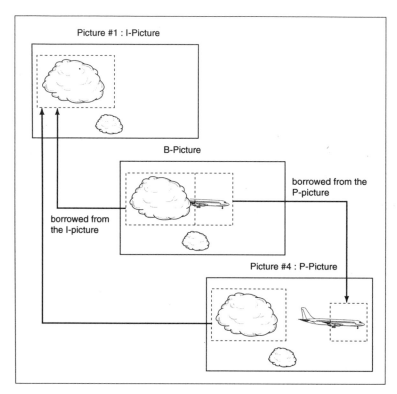

Figure 3.4: Use of a B-picture.

later reference. This makes B-pictures quite a complex feature to implement in MPEG-2 Video. Because of the described complexity of B-pictures, MPEG-2 defines subsets (profiles/levels) of its capabilities, where B-pictures are not allowed.

Sequences of pictures are grouped together to Groups of Pictures (GOPs). This can be done to support random access or editing functions. A typical, widely used GOP is the sequence IBBPBBPBBPBB.

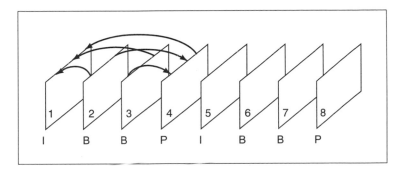

Figure 3.5: Display order of pictures.

Typically, all the B- and P-pictures of this GOP can be decoded by accessing only the I-picture or P-pictures also belonging to this GOP. This fact is indicated to editing equipment by certain bits in the GOP structure. To also support editing, the GOP structure contains a time-stamp. The timestamp format is actually defined by the Society of Motion PicTure Engineers (SMPTE) and corresponds to the timecode that is also used in other video studio equipment.

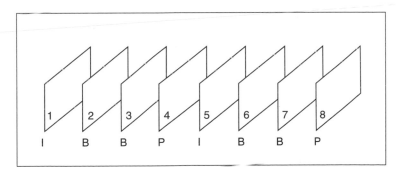

Figure 3.6: Transmission order of pictures.

Slices

Slices are elements to support random access within a picture. A slice is simply a series of macroblocks. The slice contains information about where to display the contained macroblocks on the screen. In the case of a transmission error and the loss of picture information, the information in a slice can be used to continue the display process within a picture. Instead of dropping the whole picture, the decoder can continue with the start of the next slice. To achieve high robustness against transmission errors, it would make sense to have a high number of slices per picture. On the other hand, this would mean more overhead information per picture, so a balance between error robustness and bandwidth usage needs to be maintained. Not all macroblocks of a picture must be included in slices. In this case, the slice structure is called a *general* slice structure. In a *restricted* slice structure, the whole picture is covered with slices and all macroblocks are part of a slice. From a data compression point of view, slices are not really necessary. They are only coded to have resynchronization points within the picture.

Fields

Since MPEG-2 was designed to also handle interlaced video display modes, the MPEG-2 standard's video part considers interlaced fields in the definition of pictures or macroblocks. The pictures mentioned above (I-, P-, and B-pictures) can therefore either be coded as field pictures or as frame pictures. In the first case, two *field pictures* should always occur in a pair, one containing the top field, the other containing the bottom field of the complete frame. The alternative is to first combine the fields to a frame and then encode it as a *frame picture*. Frame pictures are typically used if there is a lot of detail in the picture and only limited motion. If there is motion in the picture and not so much detail, it makes sense to use field picture coding, where the second field can be predicted from the first. In this case, the first field picture is quite a good reference to predict motion in the second field picture.

Data Compression Used in MPEG-2 Video

Actual data compression is achieved by combining three techniques:

1. Removing picture information that is invisible to the human eye: Because of its internal structure, the human eye is quite insensitive to high frequencies in color changes. The idea is, therefore, to represent the picture information in such a way that this characteristic of the eye is used. MPEG-2 uses a method, which is based on the DCT to approximate the original chrominance and luminance information in each block. Instead of using the real color values for each block, a set of frequency coefficients is calculated. This set describes the color transitions in the block.

   By dividing the resulting coefficients by a certain value, some of them can become zero after rounding. This is the step where picture information is lost. This process is called quantization and the factors are provided by a quantization matrix. MPEG-2 defines default quantization matrices, but also allows user-defined quantization matrices. Quantization is also controlled by a scale factor, which allows the user to adjust the quantization level (and by this, also the compression ratio). The scaling factor is provided for each slice and can optionally be redefined for each macroblock. This is typically done if macroblocks in a certain region of the picture do not contain a lot of detail. However, some other part of the picture can still contain a lot of detail, where high quantization cannot be used. By having the scaling factor in the quantization process, it becomes possible to generate constant bit rate video streams, which fit into the constraints that might be given by a certain network architecture. Fig. 3.7 shows the main components of the quantization process.

After the DCT process, the coefficients for increasing frequencies are distributed in a zig-zag order. This zig-zag order is matched by increasing values in the quantization matrice, as seen in Fig. 3.7. As a result, the quantization process delivers a large number of zeros in high frequency range. This is important because after scanning the resulting coefficient matrix in the same zig-zag order, it is easy to code the resulting row of numbers efficiently with variable length coding techniques. So far, only the amount of (invisible) details in the picture have been reduced by getting zero coefficients back. During decoding, these zero coefficients will prevent the inverse quantization and DCT functions to recreate the exact original signal and so cause the loss of detail. However, after the quantization, the number of values belonging to the block is still the same. For all 64 original pixel values in a block, the algorithm delivers, in total, 64 coefficients, of which some are zero. The reduction in terms of the number of bits needed to describe the blocks is

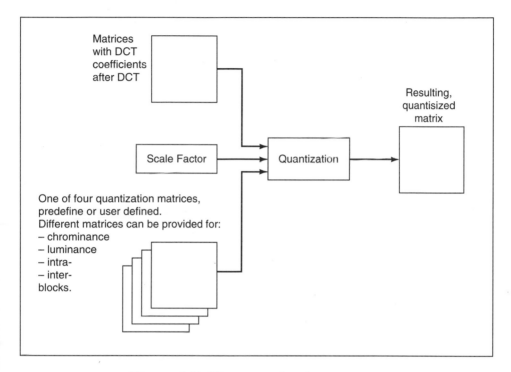

Figure 3.7: The quantization process.

achieved later with variable length coding. Since the quantization removes picture information, which can not be restored later on, the compression used in MPEG is a lossy compression technique. Fig. 3.8 shows the default quantization matrix for intra-blocks in MPEG-2 Video.

2. Using variable length coding tables: MPEG-2 defines a number of tables with codes to be used for specific patterns in a coefficient data sequence. The trick is to use very short codes (only

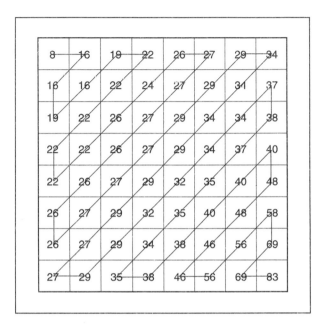

Figure 3.8: MPEG-2 Video quantization matrix.

a few bits) for patterns that ,occur very often in the sequence. As said before, the quantization process results in a number of coefficients where certain coefficients equal zero (e.g., 2,0,0, 1,0,0,1). MPEG-2 Video is coding this sequence of coefficient data by an assigned code for a specific coefficient data pattern. The interpretation of this codes gives back two values. One value specifies the number of leading zeros in front of a non-zero coefficient. MPEG-2 Video uses the term run for this value. The other value is the actual coefficient, which is called level in MPEG-2 Video. Therefore, this coding method is also known as run-level coding or Variable Length (VL) coding. An example of

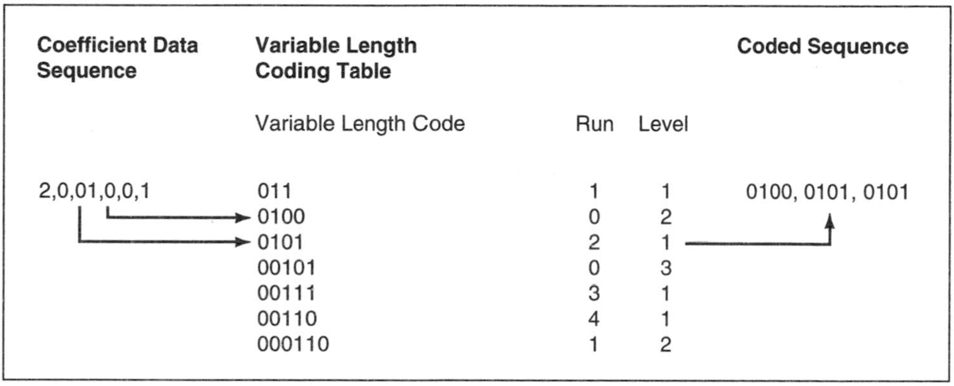

Coefficient Data Sequence	Variable Length Coding Table			Coded Sequence
	Variable Length Code	Run	Level	
2,0,01,0,0,1	011	1	1	0100, 0101, 0101
	0100	0	2	
	0101	2	1	
	00101	0	3	
	00111	3	1	
	00110	4	1	
	000110	1	2	

Figure 3.9: Variable length coding

the variable length codes and the corresponding "run" and "level" values is seen in Fig. 3.9. Based on this table the sequence described above could be represented by the code sequence "0100," "0101," and "0101." The variable length coding tables use between 2 and 13 bits to encode run-level combinations. However, not all possible combinations of run and level can be covered by the tables. For the uncovered combinations, MPEG-2 Video defines an escape coding mechanism. The level will then be coded with the actual value.

3. Motion estimation: The idea behind motion estimation is to identify regions in the picture that can be found in the following picture as well. Since the pictures occur at rates of 20-30 per second, it is very likely that similar, but maybe slightly moved, regions can be detected in adjacent pictures. The motion estimation process use the macroblocks as basic units for comparison. For each macroblock, the encoder is searching the previous

picture (in the case of a P-picture) or the previous and the future picture (in the case of a B-picture) for a macroblock that matches or closely matches the current macroblock. If such a macroblock is found, the difference between this macroblock and the current macroblock is calculated. The resulting difference is first DCT coded and then, together with the motion vector of the macroblock, VL coded. At decoding time, the motion vector is used to identify the macroblock in the previous or future picture. The identified macroblock will then be combined with the decoded difference and written into the display or future picture buffer. In the optimal case, the current macroblock is found at the same place in the previous picture. This would result in a zero motion vector together with a null difference. MPEG-2 would skip the coding of this macroblock and at decoding time the previously displayed macroblock would stay on the screen. This motion estimation concept is the reason why MPEG-2 Video can have problems encoding scenes with a lot of moving objects. A moving camera, which is following a football in front of a moving crowd of spectators, results in a sequence of pictures where it is difficult for the encoder to find similar macroblocks that are moving across the scene. In such a case, intracoding has to be used. Motion estimation also does not work in the case of scene changes or splicing because the information from one picture to the next picture changes completely at the splice. In this case, the first picture after the splice has to be intracoded.

Let's have a look on how the decoding of pictures in a display sequence IBBP would work (see also Fig. 3.10): The sequence contains

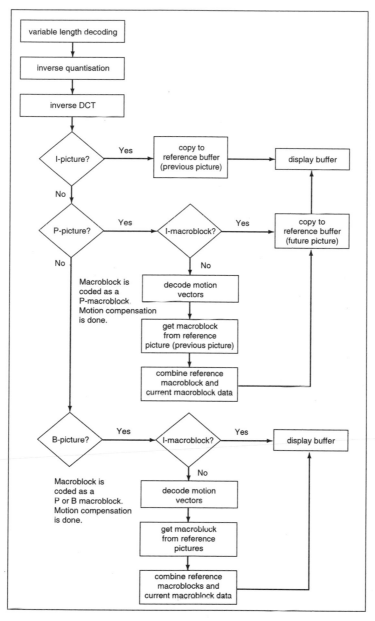

Figure 3.10: MPEG-2 decoding process.

B-pictures, so that a reordering takes place. At the decoder, the pictures arrive in the transmission sequence, which is IPBB.

The decoding of the I-picture is relatively simple. Each macroblock is decoded by decoding each of its blocks. The decoding of the block follows the three steps previously mentioned: variable length decoding, inverse quantization, and inverse DCT. In general, there is no motion prediction done in an I-picture, so that this step is skipped.[1] The resulting values are put in the display buffer and are displayed. However, a copy of the picture is also put into a buffer, which always holds the previous decoded picture.

Now the next picture comes in. It is a P-picture that is going to be displayed later, but it is needed as a reference picture for the next B-picture in the sequence.

The P-picture is decoded by using information from the previously stored I-picture. For each macroblock that was not skipped during encoding, the decoder checks if the macroblock was coded as an I-macroblock or as a P-macroblock. In the case of an I-macroblock, the macroblock is decoded, as described above, for the I-picture. If it was coded as a P-macroblock, motion compensation is finished. Motion compensation needs the motion vectors, so these are decoded first. The motion vectors are then used to access a macroblock in the previous picture. The macroblock which was retrieved is then combined with the data of the current P-macroblock structure and saved in the buffer for future pictures. Other P-macroblocks of the P-picture are decoded in

---

[1] For error robustness, I-pictures could contain so called concelament motion vectors. In this case, motion prediction is also done for I-pictures.

the same way. If the macroblock was skipped during encoding, the corresponding macroblock from the previous picture is used.

The next picture being decoded is the first of two B-pictures. The decoding works similar to the one used for the P-picture, however, the macroblock could be coded as an I-, a P-, or a B-macroblock. If the macroblock was coded as a B-macroblock, not only the I-picture, but also the just decoded P-picture can be used for motion compensation. When every coded macroblock of the first B-picture is decoded, it is displayed. The decoder then starts to decode the second B-picture, displays it, and then displays the previously decoded P-picture, which was used as a reference picture in the mean time.

3.3.3 MPEG-2 Video—The Video Bitstream Syntax

The application requirements that MPEG-2 addressed, made it necessary to develop a formal syntax that supported all requirements. The MPEG-2 Video syntax therefore became highly variable. This means that some syntax elements control the appearance of other syntax elements. Also, many syntax elements are optional and only present in the bitstream if a flag (mostly located in the syntax structure header) indicates it. By doing this, the amount of data that has to be transmitted is further reduced. Instead of transmitting void values, like zeros or special codes, some elements are simply not present in the bit stream.

The MPEG-2 standard uses a C-like pseudo-code to describe the syntax. As an example, Fig. 3.11 shows the definition of the syntax structure "video_sequence."

The MPEG-2 Video syntax makes use of pre-defined objects like basic functions and start codes. In the example, the function "nextbits()" is used to compare the next bits to be decoded with some predefined start codes. The start codes are uniquely defined in MPEG-2 Video and cannot reoccur at some other point in the bit stream. The uniqueness is guaranteed by inserting so-called "marker_bits" in the video bit stream or by forbidding certain values for some syntax elements.

Fig. 3.12 shows the MPEG-2 Video syntax hierarchy and Table 3.2 on pages 65–67 gives an overview of the contents of the most important fields in the MPEG-2 Video syntax structures. Please note that the figure only shows the hierarchy, it does not show which structures are optional or mandantory. Also, the structures can be repetitive (e.g., a video sequence can contain multiple pictures).

```
video_sequence() {
next_start_code()
sequence_header()
if (nextbits()==extension_start_code)  {
sequence_extension()
do {
     extension_and_user_data (0)
     do {
             if (nextbits()==group_start_code) {
                group_of_pictures_header()
                extension_and_user_data (1)
             }
             picture_header()
             picture_coding_extension()
             extension_and_user_data (2)
             picture_data()
     } while (( next_bits()==picture_start_code) _
             (nextbits()==group_start_code) {
     if (nextbits() !=sequence_end_code) {
             sequence_header()
             sequence_extension()
}
     } while (nextbits()  !=sequence_end_code)
} else {
     MPEG-1
}
sequence_end_code
}
```

Figure 3.11: Definition of the video
sequence in an MPEG-2 syntax.

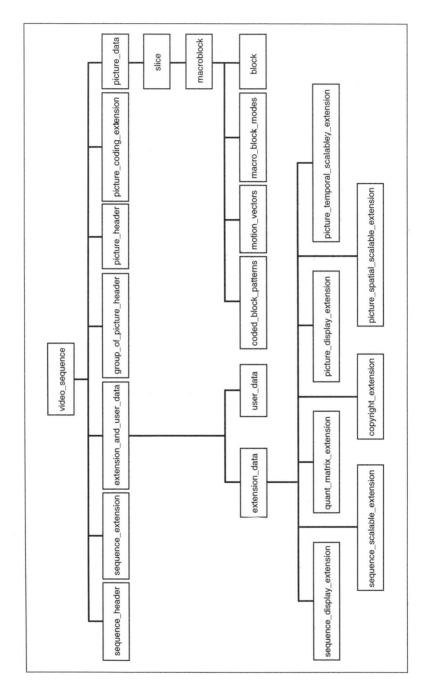

Figure 3.12: MPEG-2 video syntax hierarchy.

Syntax Structure	Content
video_sequence	Top level structure containing pictures and extension data.
sequence_header	The sequence header contains information about the picture size and frame rate. This information is used if the decoder has to synchronize a new "program" after switching from one video stream to another. Also can contain special quantization matrices, which are needed for this specific sequence of pictures.
sequence_extension	Contains profile/level and chroma format indication for this bitstream. Important: If the sequence_extension structure is not present, then the bitstream is a MPEG-1 Video bitstream.
group_of _picture_header	Contains a timecode, editing related information about the pictures enclosed in the GOP and a number of picture related structures.
picture_header	Contains an indication if the picture is an I-, P-, or B-picture. The picture header also contains a so called temporal reference field, which helps to indicate the display sequence.
picture_coding_extension	Contains additional picture information to support interlace/progressive mode and specific analog video standards (NTSC, PAL).
picture_data	Contains a number of slices. *Continued*

Table 3.2: MPEG-2 Video Syntax Structures.

Syntax Structure	Content
slice	Contains the vertical position of the slice, information to support data partitioning, the quantization scale, and a number of macroblock structures.
macroblock	Contains an optional quantization scale, blocks, macroblock_modes, and motion_vectors.
macroblock_modes	Contains indications about how the macroblock is coded. In a P-picture, the macroblock could be coded as an I-macroblock or P-macroblock. For B-pictures the macroblock mode provides information if it is coded as an I-, P-, or B-macroblock and what prediction mode is used for a B-macroblock.
motion_vectors	Contains motion vectors for the macroblock.
coded_block_pattern	In the case that all coefficients of a block are zero after the quantization, this block does not need to be coded in a macroblock that is used in a P- or B-picture. The coded block pattern therefore indicates which of the blocks in the macroblock are actually coded.
block	Contains the actual DCT coefficients.
user_ data	Contains user defined data.
sequence_display_extension	Contains additional information about the video format and color attributes used in the bitstream.
sequence_scalable_extension	Contains information about which scaleable mode is used in the video bit stream. Provides information to the decoder on how to handle the scalability. *Continued*

Table 3.2: MPEG-2 Video Syntax Structures, *Continued*

Syntax Structure	Content
quant_matrix_extension	Contains user-defined matrices for dequantisation.
picture_display_extension	Contains information to be used during the display process (e.g. to identify a window of most interest on the display).
picture_temporal_scalable_extension	Contains information to support temporal scalability.
picture_spatial_scalable_extension	Contains information to support spatial scalability.
copyright_extension	Provides information about wether the bitstream is the original or a copy. Also contains indications if the bitstream is copyright protected and provides a copyright number.

Table 3.2: MPEG-2 Video Syntax Structures, *Continued*

3.3.4 MPEG-2 Video—Scalability

Possibly one of the most important features of the MPEG-2 Video standard is the built-in support for a range of different video applications. MPEG-2 can be used for standard TV distribution, for HDTV, or for the transmission of video via telecommunication networks. Instead of defining different standards variants for all those applications and having totally different bit stream formats for the different applications, MPEG-2 uses a scaleable approach.

The scalability is achieved by the MPEG-2 Video syntax. Video information can be separated in different information streams, which are complementary to each other. Different applications can be realized just by combining different streams of information. MPEG-2 uses the term "layer" for the different information streams.

One application of the scaleable syntax concept might be the following: one layer contains the video information for a standard (PAL or NTSC resolution) TV program. This layer, called the "base layer" in MPEG-2, could then be combined with another information stream, the "enhancement layer," which contains additional video information to get a HDTV quality video. Depending on the implemented feature set in the decoder, the consumer would be able to see the standard TV or the HDTV program. However, there is only a single bit stream delivered to the home. Scalability can be applied for different aspects of video presentation, consequently the MPEG-2 Standard defines several scaleable modes.

Spatial Scalability

Spatial scalability is defined as the MPEG-2 capability to support different picture resolutions (on the X and Y axis) in a single video stream. The situation described above, where standard TV and HDTV are combined, is an example for the spatial scalability of MPEG-2. Another example would be the interworking of different digital video standards. The base layer could be encoded according to ISO/IEC 11172-2 (MPEG-1 Video) and the enhancement layer according to ISO/IEC 13818-2 (MPEG-2 Video). A software decoder could then be used to view the base layer video information and a hardware-based MPEG-2 decoder could enable the consumer to view the video with higher resolution. With spatial scalability, the enhancement layer and the base layer data is combined after the Inverse DCT step. The process mainly

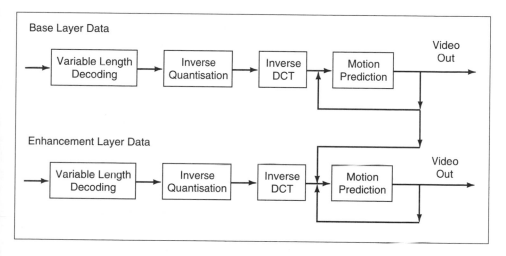

Figure 3.13: Decoding flow in the case
of spatial and temporal scalability.

affected by spatial scalability is the motion compensation, which can
now use motion vectors from the enhancement layer data or from the
base layer data. The whole decode process in the case of the spatial
scalability is illustrated in Fig. 3.13.

Temporal Scalability

Temporal scalability defines the possibility to handle different picture
rates in a single video stream. The base layer, which provides the basic
video picture, can be combined with the enhancement layer to achieve
higher frame rates. The enhancement layer uses base layer information to generate final video pictures. Possible usage is in the support of
different generations of decoder equipment or the use in networks with

69

different transmission qualities. As in the case of spatial scalability, the enhancement happens after the inverse DCT step and mainly affects the motion compensation process.

SNR Scalability

Signal to Noise Ratio (SNR) scalability allows for the handling of at least two different video qualities. The video information provided by the base layer can be improved by one or more enhancement layers carrying additional information. However, the base and enhancement layers have the same spatial video resolution. The main application of the SNR scalability is error concealment. In this case, the base layer would carry the most critical information while using a quite robust transport channel in a network. The enhancement layer, bearing the less critical, information could be transported over a transport channel with a lower quality of service. In the case of data loss in this low performance channel, the impact on the quality of the video picture would not be too obvious. The enhancement process in the case of the SNR scalability happens after the inverse quantization process. The enhancement layer contains mainly DCT coefficients, which are added to the one provided by the base layer. By doing this the picture quality is refined. Fig. 3.14 shows the data flow in the decoder if SNR scalability is used.

Data partitioning

Data partitioning can be used to split the complete video bitstream into parts with relatively higher or lower importance. The most important syntax elements are transmitted on a high performance channel, the

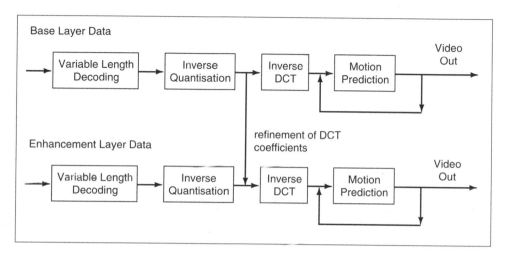

Figure 3.14: Decoding flow in the case of SNR scalability.

less important elements on a channel with lower performance. Fig. 3.15 shows an example, where, from the complete video bitstream syntax elements, all the higher layer syntax elements (like sequence headers, GOP headers, or picture headers) plus one DCT coefficient are put into the high quality channel. All the remaining coefficients are put in the other partition and could be transmitted on a "lower quality" channel. A special syntax element, called priority_breakpoint, is used to define which parts of the video bit stream syntax are put into which partition. Table 3.3 shows some values of the priority_break point and the syntax elements that are affected by this value.

A value of 1 for the priority_breakpoint would mean that the syntax elements video sequence, group_of_pictures, picture and some parts of the slice syntax are put into partition 0 (the high-priority partition). All of the remaining syntax structures (starting with the macroblock

Priority Breakpoint Value	Syntax Elements that are put into the high priority partition
1	All data in sequence header, GOP, picture, and slice to the extra_bit_slice in the slice syntax element.
2	All data above, plus macroblock data, to the macroblock address increment.
3	All data included above, plus macroblock data to coded_block_pattern.
4...63	Reserved.
64	All syntax elements to block level, including the first DCT coefficient.
65	All of the above plus 2 DCT coefficients.
63+n	All of the above plus n DCT coefficients.
127	All of the above plus 64 DCT coefficients.

Table 3.3: Priority breakpoint values.

structure and going down in the hierarchy) would be placed into Partition 1. A value of 64 would indicate that the first coefficient and all syntax elements hierarchally above the DCT coefficients are put into Partition 0. The remaining coefficients are put into Partition 1. Fig. 3.15 shows this last example. A decoder that is able to handle data partitioning would first decode the bitstream delivered on Partition 0 and then switch over to Partition 1 to process the remaining syntax structures.

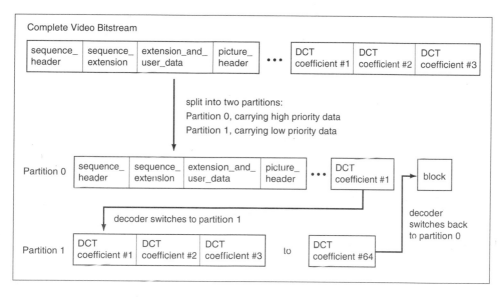

Figure 3.15: Decoding flow in the case of data partitioning.

3.3.5 MPEG-2 Video—
Profiles and Levels

Because of the great range of applications MPEG-2 is intended to address, the standard became quite complex. However, an application might not need the full range of the MPEG-2 Video feature set. MPEG-2 equipment would be prohibitively expensive if it had to support the complete specification. Therefore, the standard defines so called *profiles* and *levels* to define subsets of MPEG-2 Video. MPEG-2 defines the following profiles and levels in Table 3.4.

Profiles	Levels
Simple Profile (SP)	Low Level (LL)
Main Profile (MP)	Main Level (ML)
SNR Scaleable Profile (SNR)	High 1440 Level (H14)
Spatial Scaleable Profile (Spatial)	High Level (HL)
High Profile (HP)	

Table 3.4: Profiles and levels defined by MPEG-2 Video.

A profile is described as a well defined subset of the video syntax. Certain syntax elements defined by MPEG-2 Video are not valid and cannot be decoded if the decoder only supports a "low" profile.

For instance, the "simple" profile does not support B-pictures and neither the "simple" nor the "main" profile supports any kind of scalability. However, the "lower" profiles are always a subset of the "higher" profiles. A decoder supporting the spatial profile is required to support spatial and SNR scalability. Some of the constraints for the different profiles are shown in Table 3.5.

A level defines values for certain parameters in the video bit stream. For instance, the levels describe the number of samples per line, the number of lines per frame and the number of frames per second. Profiles and levels are combined to exactly define which selection or subset from the MPEG-2 Video toolkit is used. A very important combination is the "Main Level at Main Profile" (ML @ MP) combination. This combination defines a sufficient subset of the MPEG-2 Video functionality,

MPEG-2 feature	Simple Profile	Main Profile	SNR Profile	Spatial Profile	High Profile
Chroma Format	4:2:0	4:2:0	4:2:0	4:2:0	4:2:2 or 4:2:0
Picture Type	I,P	I,P,B	I,P,B	I,P,B	I,P,B
Scaleable	No	No	Yes	Yes	Yes
Scaleable Mode	None	None	SNR	SNR or spatial	SNR or spatial
Spatial scaleable mode	No	No	No	Yes	Yes

Table 3.5: MPEG-2 profile constraints.

so that standard TV broadcast, in PAL or NTSC quality, can be realized. Table 3.6 shows some of the ML @ MP parameter values.

Profiles and levels are organized hierarchically and MPEG-2 Video defines a forward compatibility between different profiles and levels. A decoder supporting a high profile must also support the appropriate lower profile[2]. The forward compatibility, which decoders must follow, is shown in Table 3.7.

---

[2]There is one exception to this rule, which is that a Simple Profile @ Main Level decoder should also be able to decode Main Profile @ Low Level bitstreams.

Parameter	ML@MP value
samples/line	720
lines/frame	576
frames/sec	30
luminance samples/sec	10,368,000
max. video data rate in Mbit/s	15
max size of decoder buffer (bits)	1,835,008

Table 3.6: MPEG-2 main level—main profile values.

	Decoder supporting:										
Profile and Level of bit stream	HP @ HL	HP @ H14	HP @ ML	Spatial @ H14	SNR @ ML	SNR @ LL	MP @ HL	MP @ H14	MP @ ML	MP @ LL	SP @ ML
HP@HL	X										
HP@H14	X	X									
HP@ML	X	X	X								
Spatial @H14	X	X		X							
SNR@ML	X	X	X	X	X						
SNR@LL	X	X	X	X	X	X					
MP@HL	X						X				
MP@H14	X	X		X			X	X			
MP@ML	X	X	X	X	X		X	X	X		
MP@LL	X	X	X	X	X	X	X	X	X	X	X
SP@ML	X	X	X	X	X		X	X	X		X
MPEG-1	X	X	X	X	X	X	X	X	X	X	X

Table 3.7: Decoder compatibility chart.

3.4 MPEG Audio

3.4.1 Introduction

The aim of this section is to provide an overview of the most important aspects in audio compression and coding techniques utilized in MPEG-2. Analogous to what we have experienced by studying the manipulation of the video signal, the resulting compression and encoding of the audio signal is extremely powerful, and yet at the same time very flexible. The standards describing MPEG-1 and -2 audio coding are ISO/IEC 11172-3 and ISO/IEC 13818-3 respectively. Note that as for the MPEG-2 Video compression, MPEG does not define the encoder models, it only defines the bitstream format and a reference decoder model.

The audio part of the MPEG-2 standard is to a great extent based on the MPEG-1 audio part, and a great deal of compatibility exists. The compatibility aspect is valid in two ways: in the sense that existing MPEG-1 equipment can make a partial decode of MPEG-2 signals by extracting the MPEG-1 compatible part ("Backwards Compatibility"), and in the sense that MPEG-2 equipment can decode MPEG-1 signals ("Forwards Compatibility"). As a consequence, it makes little sense to study MPEG-2 Audio processing without first understanding MPEG-1 audio processing.

3.4.2 Layers 1, 2, and 3

MPEG-1, as well as MPEG-2, audio compression describes three degrees of compression—Layers 1, 2, and 3. The level of compression, the demands for processing power, and the sound quality all increase proportionally with the layer number. The required transmission bandwidth in contrast, decreases with the layer number. Layer 1 has the lowest compression rate—about four times—it demands the smallest amount of processing power, and has the lowest delay (realistically below 50 ms). Layer 1 also has the highest requirements for transmission bandwidth, as it has an output bit rate of between 32 Kbps in mono, with the highest possible level of compression—going to 448 Kbps in stereo, with the lowest possible level of compression. The sound quality of the Layer 1 signal is furthermore inferior to what can be obtained by Layers 2 and 3.

At the other end, Layer 3 is intended to yield the best sound quality of the three layers, while it achieves a compression rate of a factor 1:10. The processing time is on the other hand also more than 3 times longer. See Table 3.8 for the most important characteristics of these three layers.

These three layers are compatible in the sense that a layer N decoder can decode layer N, as well as all the layers below. For instance, a Layer 3 decoder can decode Layers 1, 2, and 3 bit streams, but a Layer 2 decoder can only decode bit streams from Layers 1 and 2.

The reason for having more than just one universal layer to address all needs is based partly on need and partly on history. First of all, it is necessary to consider the application. If, for instance, high-quality audio reproduction at low bit rate is a key requirement, and processing power/cost is of secondary importance, then Layer 3 would make a logical choice.

The development of the layers has furthermore been a gradual process. Layer 3 specifications were finished later than Layers 1 and 2. This means that for some time, only Layer 1 and 2 compliant equip-

Layer	Approximate Compression Rate (@ target bit rate)	Target Bit Rate	Allowed Bit Rate Range (MPEG-1)	Realistic Delay	Theoretical Minimum Delay
1	1:4	192 Kbps	32–448 Kbps	< 50 ms	19 ms
2	1:6	128 Kbps	32– 384 Kbps	100 ms	35 ms
3	1:10	64 Kbps	32–320 Kbps	150 ms	58 ms

Table 3.8: Central characteristics
of the three layers of MPEG audio coding.

ment had been produced, which again led to the fact that significant know-how in the use of Layers 1 and 2 has been gained in the industry, leaving these layers as the most used.

3.4.3 MPEG Audio Compression and Encoding

All three layers in MPEG-1 have certain compression and encoding techniques in common. The following is an overall introduction to the structure and function of this process. The diagram seen in Fig. 3.16 shows the process taking place. A short description of each major function will follow.

The input to the process is a digital audio signal, which first enters the *filter bank* process, as seen in Fig. 3.16. (In the case of signals with more than one audio channel, as with stereo sound for instance, each

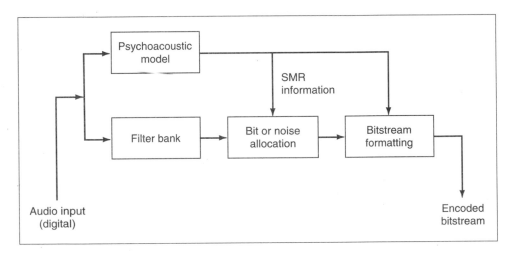

Figure 3.16: The overall audio compression
and encoding process for all three layers.

channel is treated separately.) The filter bank used in MPEG audio coding can be of two types, either a so called polyphase, or a hybrid polyphase and MDCT. Regardless of the type, the time domain samples are here converted into the same number of frequency domain samples. The output of the filter bank is a number of sub-bands of equal bandwidth. In Layers 1 and 2 a filter bank yielding 32 sub-bands, each containing 12 or 36 frequency domain samples respectively, is used. In Layer three, the number of sub-bands can be either 192 or 576.

In parallel with the filter bank, the *psychoacoustic model* process calculates the signal to mask ratio (SMR) for each sub-band. The principal function of the psychoacoustic model is to calculate a new bit allocation for the frequency samples in the sub-bands. The new bit allocation is aimed at efficiently allocating the available bits to each of the subbands. Therefore, if there is no power in a given sub-band, no bits are allocated. The central principle applied is the fact that frequencies with higher power makes nearby frequencies of lower power inaudible to the human hearing, as explained in Section 2.3. The new bit allocation is calculated separately for each sub-band.

To obtain the SNR, it is necessary to first make a time to frequency domain conversion of the original audio signal. (Note that this works in parallel with the filter bank process.) This conversion is done by the Fast Fourier Transformation technique (FFT), which allows a time to frequency domain transformation with a better spectral resolution than that of the polyphase filter bank. On the basis of the frequency domain data, the maximum power in each sub-band is found, the tonal and non-tonal (noise like) parts of the audio signal is determined, the absolute masking threshold (the threshold in quietness) is identified, and, finally, the masking thresholds of all the individual sub-bands are calculated. A global masking threshold is thereafter calculated by adding all the individual masking thresholds with the absolute threshold. For each sub-band it is now possible to calculate the difference between the actual signal and the masking threshold, and obtain the signal to mask ratio.

The *bit or noise allocation* process uses the output samples from the filter bank and the SMR information from the psychoacoustic model to determine the amount of quantisation noise that is tolerable in each sub-band (i.e., the noise level that is covered by the level of the original audio signal). This is shown in Fig. 3.17. Consequently, the number of quantisation steps (i.e., the number of bits per sample) necessary to use in each sub-band can be determined. The higher the allowable quantisation noise, the lower the number of necessary bits to represent each sample. In layer 1 a scalefactor is applied for each

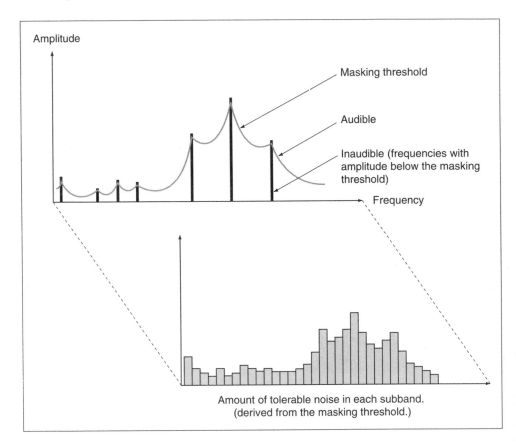

Figure 3.17: Calculated masking threshold
and the allowable levels of noise in each sub-band.

sub-band (containing 12 audio samples). In Layer 2, each sub-band contains 36 audio samples, which are split into three groups of 12 samples. Each of the three groups can—but do not necessarily—have separate scalefactors.

The so called scalefactors are calculated separately for each sub-band. The scalefactor, which will be transmitted along with the audio samples to the decoder, expresses a certain factor that the resolution steps of the audio samples will have to be multiplied by on the decoder side. It is hereby possible to express small as well as large amplitude steps with a relatively small number of bits.

The total output of the bit or noise allocation process must meet a fixed bit rate, the target bit rate. At the same time, the encoder tries to meet the resolution/masking requirements, set forth by the psychoacoustic model in order not to lower the perceived audio quality at a given moment. (The specific bit rate is initially specified to the encoder.)

For Layers 1 and 2, the number of bits used to represent the audio samples in each sub-band is the variable, when the requirements of the bit rate and those of the psychoacoustic model are to be combined. In Layer 3, this is done somewhat differently, as it is noise injected in the sub-bands, which is the variable. In both cases, the encoder starts an iterative process of increasing the accuracy of the sub-band quantisation, to the limit possible within the specified bit rate.

In the *bitstream formatting* process, the sub-band frequency samples, the bit allocation for Layers 1 and 2 (in the case of Layer 3, the noise allocation), are joined together with the scalefactor information in the audio data field of the audio frame. Furthermore, the audio frame contains header, error check, and ancillary data fields, as can be seen in the illustration of the PDU structure in Fig. 3.18. For Layer 3, Huffmann encoding of the quantized frequency samples is applied at this step. This means that instead of fixed length PCM[3] code for each frequency sample, as used in Layers 1 and 2, a variable length code is

---

[3]Pulse Code Modulation.

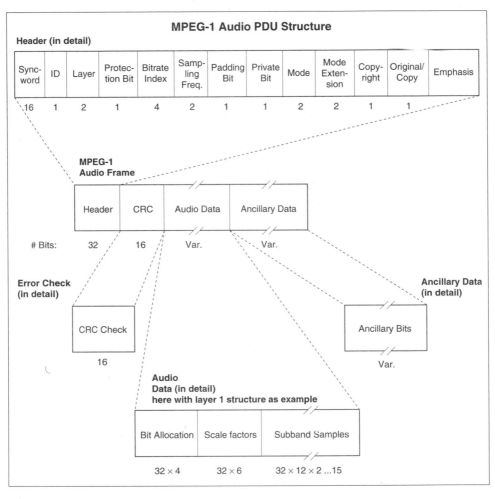

Figure 3.18: PDU structure of the MPEG-1 Audio frame.

used. Huffman coding represents the most common bit combinations in the data flow, with the shortest codes, and the most uncommon, with the longest codes. Hereby, further reduction in the bit rate can be obtained.

PDU structure

The PDU structure found in MPEG audio coding is split into four major parts. The header, the error check field, the audio data field, and the ancillary data field. The header structure is common to all three layers in MPEG-1 and MPEG-2. The CRC check is enabled if the "protection bit" in the header is equal to 0. The 16 bits of the error check field will then contain a parity check word, to enable error detection in the bit stream. The audio data field contains the actual frequency domain samples, along with the necessary additional information. The example of Fig. 3.18 shows the structure found in Layer 1. Here, the information for bit allocation and scalefactors for each of the 32 sub-bands precedes the actual frequency domain audio samples. Note that in Layer 1 there are 12 audio samples for each of the 32 sub-bands, and the samples can be represented by between 2 and 15 bits, according to what is necessary after calculating the masking effect and the SMR. For Layers 2 and 3, the PDU structure in the audio data field is different, reflecting the more complex compression and coding technique found in these layers. The ancillary data field can carry additional information of various kinds if needed. Its length is therefore not defined. It is this field that carries the major part of additional information needed for multi-channel sound, as found in MPEG-2. More details of the PDU fields shown in Fig. 3.18 can be found in Table 3.9. Note that the structures used in Layers 2 and 3 of the audio data field are not described.

PDU field	Description
Syncword	Allows decoder to synchronize upon beginning of the frame. Always set to all "1"s.
ID	Indicates if the PDU is coded according to MPEG-1 or MPEG-2.
Layer	Indicates the layer used. Layer 1, 2, or 3.
Protection Bit	Indicates if error check is present.
Bit Rate Index	Indicates the bit rate used, regardless of the mode (single channel, stereo etc.). Fourteen discrete steps are specified in MPEG-1 ranging from 32 to 448 Kbps in Layer 1, from 32 to 384 Kbps in Layer 2 and from 32 to 320 Kbps in Layer 3. In MPEG-2, the 14 discrete steps cover the range 32 to 256 Kbps in Layer 1, and 8 to 160 Kbps for Layers 2 and 3.
Sampling Freq.	Indicates the sampling frequency used: 32, 44.1, or 48 KHz in MPEG-1, or 16, 22.05 or 24 KHz in MPEG-2.
Padding Bit	Indicates whether padding is present or not. (Can be needed to adjust output to specified mean bit rate).
Private Bit	The use is not specified by ISO/IEC.

Table 3.9: The MPEG-1—and to some extent,
the MPEG-2—Audio PDU structure.

PDU field	Description
Mode	Indicates mode used. Stereo, intensity stereo and/or MS stereo, dual channel (two independent channels) or single channel.
Mode Extension	Used in "Intensity stereo and /or MS stereo" mode (note differences between use, according to layer).
	Layers 1 & 2: Specifies which sub-bands are coded in intensity stereo. (All others are coded in normal stereo.) The following ranges of sub-bands can be coded in intensity stereo: 4-31, 8-31, 12-31, or 16-31.
	Layer 3: Specifies the used combination of intensity stereo and MS-stereo. The following combinations are possible: neither intensity or MS stereo are used, only intensity stereo is used, only MS stereo is used, or both intensity and MS stereo are used.
Copyright	Indicates if bitstream is copyright protected or not.
Original/Copy	Indicates if bitstream is the original or a copy.
Emphasis	Indicates the type of de-emphasis that must be applied to the signal on the decoder side.
	Continued

Table 3.9: The MPEG-1—and to some extent,
the MPEG-2—Audio PDU structure, *Continued*.

87

PDU field	Description
	Error Check:
CRC Check	If "protection bit" field in header is equal to 0, this field is present. It protects the fields of the PDU most vulnerable to bit errors via a Cyclic Redundancy Check (CRC). The specific fields varies with use of MPEG-1 or -2, and the layer used. Among other parts, bits 16-31 of the header is always protected in all three layers, and in Layers 1 and 2 the bit allocation field is always protected.
	Audio Data: (MPEG-1, Layer 1)
Bit Allocation	Indicates the number of bits used to represent the samples in each sub-band, of each channel. Can take all values between 0 and 15 bits resolution per sample.
Scale Factors	Indicates the factor the samples in each sub-band, in each channel, shall be multiplied by when decoding; 63 discrete steps have been defined.
Subband Samples	Contains the actual audio samples of all sub bands, in all channels.
	Ancillary Data:
Ancillary Bits	User definable. In MPEG-2, used to carry the multi channel extension information.

Table 3.9: The MPEG-1—and to some extent,
the MPEG-2—Audio PDU structure, *Continued.*

Coding Modes

As indicated in the PDU description above, there is a range of different ways to utilize the transmission capabilities of the channels available in MPEG audio coding. The four different coding modes shown in Table 3.10 are used both in MPEG-1 and MPEG-2.

The first three coding modes are fairly straight forward, whereas the fourth "joint stereo" may appear unfamiliar. Intensity stereo is designed in order to lower the bit rate somewhat, and thereby get a better compression ratio. In reality, the reduction in bit rate is between 10 and 30 Kbps. At the encoder, the two stereophonic signals are combined into one monophonoc signal in the high frequency range (the exact range of sub-bands can vary). To achieve a more realistic stereo

Ch. Utilization	Description
Mono (Single)	One monophonic signal transmitted.
Mono (Dual)	Two independent monophonic signals transmitted.
Stereo	One stereophonic signal transmitted (left/ right audio channel transmitted separately).
Joint Stereo (Intensity stereo and/or MS stereo)	One stereophonic signal is transmitted, but left and right channelinformation above a certain frequency (sub-band) is combined in order to compress the signal further.

Table 3.10: The different types of channel utilization in MPEG audio.

representation, the scalefactors for the different sub-bands are still encoded independently in the two stereo channels, so a pseudo-stereophonic signal can hereby be created at the decoder side. The above mentioned can be used in Layers 1 and 2. In Layer 3, a combination of intensity and a "sum-difference" coding technique called "MS stereo" can be used. In MS stereo, one channel carries the difference between the left and the right side signal (L-R), and the other channel carries the sum (L+R).

3.4.4 MPEG-2 Audio Additions

As mentioned, MPEG-2 Audio processing relies heavily on MPEG-1 Audio. The following gives an overview of some of the major differences and enhancements found in MPEG-2.

- **Half sample rate enhancement**
  With MPEG-2, it is possible to use only 1/2 of the sampling rate used in MPEG-1 and still obtain a very good sound quality. This is especially interesting for applications such as commentary channels, multi lingual channels and multimedia, where the full frequency span from 20 Hz to 20 KHz is seldom used anyway. This low sampling rate extension, available in MPEG-2, allows the sampling of the time domain signal to be done with 16, 22.05 or 24 K samples per second, for all three layers. This gives an upper frequency limit of 7.5, 10.3 and 11.25 KHz respectively. With the low sample rate extension, the bitrates goes down to as far as 8 Kbps for Layers 2 and 3, and 32 Kbps for Layer 1.

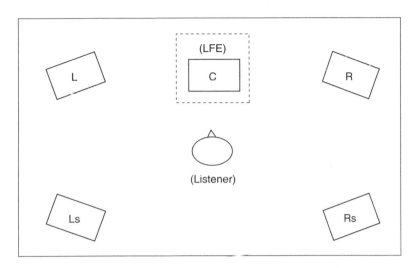

Figure 3.19: Surround sound setup in "3/2 stereo."

If the low sample rate extension is used, it is specified by the "ID" bit set to "0," as seen in Table 3.9.

- **Multi-channel extension**
  To allow transmission of more realistic stereophonic representation, MPEG-2 supports 5 audio channels, which together can convey a "surround" stereo image. The 5 channels are left channel (L), right channel (R), center channel (C), left rear surround channel (LS) and right rear surround channel (RS). This is also called "3/2 stereo" as it makes use of 3 front loudspeakers and 2 in the rear. See Fig. 3.19. In addition a low frequency enhancement (LFE) channel is available for a sub woofer signal in the range from 15 to 120 Hz. This channel is mainly used for special effects.

There are possibilities other than the 3/2 configuration described above, both on the encoder and on the decoder side. Table 3.11 shows what channels the encoder can use as input.

Combination #	# of channels	Configuration	Channels
1	5	3/2	L, R, C, LS, RS
2	5	3/0 + 2/0	L, R, C of programme #1, L2, R2 of programme #2
3	4	3/1	L, R, C and S (one surround sound channel)
4	4	2/2	L, R, LS, RS (no center channel)
5	4	2/0 + 2/0	L, R, L2, R2 (left and right channel of 2 different programmes)
6	3	3/0	L, R, C (no sorround sound)
7	3	2/1	L, R, S (left and right channel, plus one surround sound channel.)
8	2	2/0	L, R (or dual channel mode)
9	1	1/0	Mo (single mono channel)

Table 3.11: Possible input combinations to the audio encoder.

For the decoder, the channels described above can be decoded and reproduced in the combinations shown in Table 3.12. Note that the LFE channel can be used with any of these configurations as an option.

An alternative configuration of the five channel system of MPEG-2 Audio is the application of multilingual/commentary channels, accompanying a specific program with, for example, bilingual comments or sound tracks. The MPEG-2 specifications allows for up to seven multilingual/commentary channels per program.

Combination #	# of channels	Config-uration	Front Channels	Rear Channels
1	5	3/2	L, R, C	LS, RS
2	4	3/1	L, R, C	S (one surround channel)
3	4	2/2	L, R	LS, RS
4	3	2/1	L, R	S (one surround channel)
5	3	3/0	L, R, C	(No surround sound)
6	2	2/0	L, R	(No surround sound)
7	1	1/0	MO (Mono)	(No surround sound)

Table 3.12: The seven possible configurations that the MPEG-2 decoder can present.

Compatibility and Matrixing

The aspect of compatibility between MPEG-1 and MPEG-2 Audio has taken a very high priority during the work with the audio part of the MPEG-2 standard. The reason for this is mainly to speed user acceptance by ensuring that MPEG-1-based products can operate in a satisfactory manner with MPEG-2 signals, and vice versa. A MPEG-1 decoder cannot decode MPEG-2 half sample rate signals though, and it cannot fully handle all of the new options, such as LFE and surround sound, included in the MPEG-2 encoded signal. The basic frame format used in MPEG-2 Audio coding is the same as the one used in MPEG-1. The Audio Data fields carrying L and R channel information in MPEG-1 does in MPEG-2—as explained below—carry a compatible mixed signal in these fields in MPEG-2. The ancillary data field found in the MPEG-1 frame structure is used to carry the multi-channel extension information in MPEG-2.

In the case of 3/2 stereo, for instance, the challenge looks like this: One has to transmit five channels of audio information to utilize the potential of the MPEG-2 decoders. At the same time, it must be possible for MPEG-1 decoders to reproduce a signal of high quality. The solution is to mix the five channels of surround sound information into the two channels that the MPEG-1 decoder can handle by default as left and right channel information, and that MPEG-2 can use in reconstructing the full surround sound signal. This is known as matrixing and dematrixing. These two "universal" channels are called Lo and Ro, and are essentially composed in the MPEG-2 Audio encoder.[4]

---

[4]Lo and Ro are defined as follows:

$$Lo = L + aC + bLs$$
$$Ro = R + aC + bRs$$

"a and b": specific given constants describing the weighting of the added center channel and surround channel information.

In total, one can now identify seven different audio channels: L, Ls, Lo, R, Rs, Ro, and C. Lo and Ro are, as mentioned, by default transmitted in the compatible part of the MPEG 1/2 audio frame, and the last three channels are transmitted in the ancillary data fields. There are, as shown in Table 3.13, eight different combinations possible for the encoder on the three channels that the encoder can use.

All five surround channels can, in principle, be derived from any combination of Lo and Ro, and one of the combinations seen above. The choice does however depend on what combination yields the lowest bit rate, and at the same time practically allows the recovery of all five channels at the decoder side. In practice, the encoder chooses the multichannel extension channels with the lowest energy level, the ones with the lowest scalefactors. The same basic technique is applied for other

Combination number	Ch. # 1	Ch. # 2	Ch. # 3
1	L	R	C
2	L	R	Ls
3	L	Rs	C
4	L	Rs	Ls
5	L	R	Rs
6	Ls	R	C
7	Ls	R	Rs
8	Ls	Rs	C

Table 3.13: The eight combinations of channels (in the 3/2 configuration).

channel configurations such as 3/1, 3/0, 2/2, etc. The number of combinations are naturally smaller than with the 3/2 configuration, as explained above.

The "trick" of matrixing/dematrixing has the drawback that it only works if the multi-channel extension signals are the same on the dematrixing side as well as on the matrixing side. This is, unfortunately, not the case, as quantisation takes place between matrixing and dematrixing. Quantisation errors (noise) are therefore introduced from all of the multi-channel extension signals. An attempt to solve this problem is to use pre-distortion, also called pre-quanitsation. This simply means that the signals used in the matrixing process are already quantized before the matrixing takes place. The total quantisation noise is hereby lowered in the matrix/dematrix process.

Adaptive Multichannel Prediction

The surround sound signal consists of five channels, as described earlier. A great deal of redundancy often exists between these five channels, so in many cases the same piece of audio information may appear in two or more of the five surround channels with different delays. The MPEG-2 Audio compression can use this redundancy to achieve a better compression rate. In practice, the three channels carried in the multi-channel extension field may be predicted from the MPEG-1 compatible pair, Lo and Ro. The prediction process can take place independently for each of the lower eight sub-bands in the three extension channels. When the prediction functionality is used, the encoder transmits information that describes a prediction coefficient, a prediction error, and a delay compensation, instead of the actual signal in the extension channels. With this information, the encoder can reproduce the signal in the extension channels from Lo and Ro.

3.4.5 The NBC Work Group

As explained, the audio part of the MPEG-2 standard has focused on compatibility with MPEG-1 audio. The compatibility does however have some drawbacks. The matrixing/dematrixing techniques just described have not been able to completely eliminate the fact that there is a trade-off between maintaining compatibility and achieving optimal sound quality at a given bit rate. Listening tests have proved the backward compatible coding techniques to be somewhat inferior to other non-backward compatible techniques (under the condition that the same number of bits per second were available). For example, non-backward compatible methods do not suffer from the problem that quantisation noise from the matrix/dematrix process may lower the perceived sound quality.

As a consequence, a "Non-Backward Compatible" (NBC) working group, has been formed. The goal is to define an NBC audio coding technique for use with MPEG-2, which achieves higher audio quality at equivalent bitrates.

3.5 MPEG-2 Systems

3.5.1 Introduction

The video and the audio part of the MPEG-2 standard defines the format with which audio or video information is represented. However, to use this data in a complete video delivery chain some additional requirements have to be addressed. These requirements result from the applications in which the audio and video data is used in, but they are also related to the technology that is used to deliver the data.

Let's take the standard TV broadcasting application as an example. In TV broadcasting, there is a need to transport different programs to the consumer, who can freely choose between them. In other words, at some point different video/audio streams have to be multiplexed together and have to be delivered together to the consumer. This multiplexing is usually done somewhere in TV broadcasting networks, like satellite or cable distribution systems. In the case of a satellite distribution system, different programs, delivered by different broadcasting stations, are multiplexed together at some satellite uplink station. This collection of programs (sometimes also called a *bouquet*) is then transmitted to the satellite, which then sends it down to earth in a direct to the home (DTH broadcasting) system.

This multiplexing could, in principle, be a function of the underlying delivery network (e.g., if ATM networks are used, different virtual channels could be used for different programs. Please see Chapter 4 for an introduction to the ATM concept). This would, however, give a high dependency between the used network technology and the transported data.

For this reason, the ISO/IEC decided to develop their own specification; a specification that describes how the encoded audio and video bitstreams should be multiplexed together to form actual programs. The goal was to create a relatively generic specification, in order to make MPEG-coded material usable in different network and media environments. It should be independent of the network's physical implementation and should be suitable for error-free and error-prone environments. Furthermore, it should become more or less self-consistent, containing all the necessary information to decode the audio and video bitstreams belonging to a specific program.

This goal was achieved with the systems part of MPEG-2.[5] It forms a very important part of the MPEG-2 standard set and is especially important if digital video has to be delivered (e.g., via broadband networks). Fig. 3.20 shows the scope of the MPEG-2 Systems part in relation to the video and audio part and the broadband network equipment. Because the key functionality addressed by MPEG-2 Systems is multiplexing, it is sometimes referred to as the *MPEG-2 multiplex*.

MPEG-2 Systems (and also MPEG-2 Video to some extent) are using data structures that are commonly referred to as packets in the data communication world. Packets always consist of a packet header and the packet payload and can be of fixed or variable size. The basic idea behind a packet concept is to create a flexible mechanism to transport any kind of data. Usually the packet header contains the information that is needed to process the data in the packet payload (e.g., the picture type in the header of a picture packet). Depending on the application scenario the packets are used in, it makes sense to use variable

---

[5]ISO/IEC Information Technology—Generic coding of moving pictures and associated audio. Systems: ISO/IEC 13818-1.

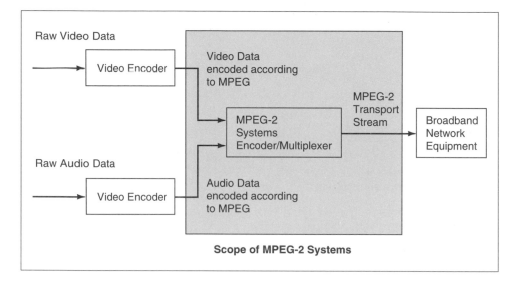

Figure 3.20: Scope of MPEG-2 Systems specifications.

or fixed sized packets. In a network environment for example, it is useful to have fixed size packets that are relatively short. This helps to optimize the network equipment that is processing the packets, because the length of the packet is always the same. Also, if a part of the packet is corrupted for some reason (e.g., by a loss of data in the network), only little information is lost. Because of the packet concept, MPEG and other transmission formats for digital video are sometimes referred as *packet video*.

The MPEG-2 System's part can be regarded as "the glue" between the video and audio technology on one side and the broadband networking world on the other. This chapter will give an introduction to the main concepts and elements of the MPEG-2 Systems part.

3.5.2 Transport Streams and Program Streams

Typically, there are two ways of delivering video information to the user. Currently, if one watches a movie, it is done either via a VCR or via broadcasted TV, where the movie is transmitted to our TV set via cable, satellite, or terrestrial broadcasting. In the case of the VCR, a local media-based delivery system, the video cassette, is used. In the case of broadcasted TV, a network-based delivery system is used. The same concept, media or network, can be applied for a video that is presented in MPEG-2. One way would be to store the video locally on a hard-disc or CD-ROM and retrieve it from this media at presentation time. The other way would be to have the video information delivered via a network and display video pictures in real time. The systems part of the MPEG-2 standard addresses both ways, which of course have different requirements to the technology that is used for the implementation. The MPEG standard defines two basic tools to support media and network delivery systems: The *program stream* and the *transport stream*.

The program stream is mainly focused on using CD-ROM and hard-disc media, while the transport stream is used in the networked environment. The program stream uses long data structures to transport video and audio data. This can only be done in "low-error environments," since a loss of any of those structures could result in serious problems with the quality of the audio and video information transfer. The transport stream uses fixed length, relatively short data structures that can be well processed in a networked environment. Since this book is about digital video in broadband networks, it will only focus on the transport stream.

One of the most important features of the transport stream is the capability to multiplex and demultiplex different programs, consisting of different video- and audio-bitstreams. Generally, the systems layer of MPEG-2 provides the necessary functionality to:

- Extract a single program out of a single transport stream, containing a collection of programs.

- Extract a subset of programs out of a single transport stream, containing a collection of programs.

- Create a single transport stream, containing a collection of programs out of several transport streams.

The synchronization has to be maintained between audio and video streams during these multiplexing processes. This is done by adding timestamp information in the transport stream data elements.

The information streams that are multiplexed together are not limited to be only audio and video bitstreams. MPEG-2 Systems also allow user defined bitstreams, the so called *private data* bitstream. An example for Private Data could be a network protocol data like TCP/IP protocol data units (PDUs). After demultiplexing the MPEG-2 transport stream in the end user equipment, the audio and video bitstreams would be decoded by the audio and video decoders, the private data would be processed by some TCP/IP protocol software.

Besides the multiplexing function, the MPEG-2 System's encoder/ multiplexer also adds control and management information to the different video and audio bitstreams. Some of the packet headers also contain CRC fields, priority bits, or error indicators. However, there

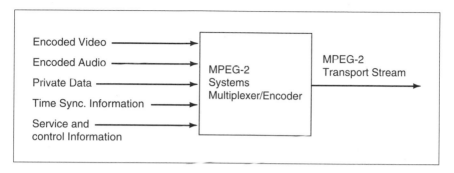

Figure 3.21: MPEG-2 System's layer processor.

is no error recovery built into the transport stream. This kind of functionality has to be handled by network protocols, which can make use of the indicators delivered by the MPEG-2 Systems layer. Fig. 3.21 summarizes the functionality of the MPEG-2 Systems layer processor.

In MPEG-2, the output bitstream of a video/audio encoder or the private data bit stream is called the *elementary stream*. In the case of audio or video, this elementary stream can be organized into *access units*. An access unit is a picture, in the case of a video elementary stream, or an audio frame, in the case of an audio elementary stream.

An elementary stream is then converted into a *packetized elementary stream,* which consist of *PES packets*. Each PES packet consists of the PES packet payload (which is a variable-sized part of the elementary stream) and a PES packet header. By having the size of the payload variable, the payload of the PES packets can be an exact access unit of the elementary stream.

The PES packet is then mapped into MPEG-2 *transport stream packets (TSP)*, also consisting of a header and a payload part. Consecu-

tive transport packets form the MPEG-2 transport stream.[6] Fig. 3.22
shows the relationship between the different data elements. If the data
of a PES packet is not completely filling the transport packet, the transport packet is filled up with stuffing bytes (hex FF). The start of the
next PES packet is then put into the next transport packet. This helps
the video decoder easily synchronize on the PES header, which now
always occurs at the start of the transport packet payload.

At first glance it seems to be strange to segment the elementary
stream into packets and then put these packets into some other packets. However, both layers were created with different objectives in
mind. The PES packet headers are adding additional information
directly related to the elementary stream (e.g., the type of the stream
[audio or video], scrambling, or copyright information). This information is, in general, independent from the used delivery mechanismen.
The transport stream packet header on the other hand provides information that is used to transport and deliver the stream. This includes
tools to multiplex different information streams. We will look at both
the transport stream packet header and the PES packet header in more
detail later in this chapter.

MPEG-2 Systems distinguish between two kinds of transport
streams:

- *Single Program Transport Streams* (SPTS): The single program transport stream contains different PES streams,
  which all share a common time base. The different PES
  streams could carry video, different audio, and perhaps

---

[6]Since packetized elementary streams are used in both the transport streams and
the program streams,a conversion between transport stream and program stream can
be realized on the PES level. A MPEG-2 System's layer processor could extract the
PES packets out of the transport stream and put them into program stream packs.

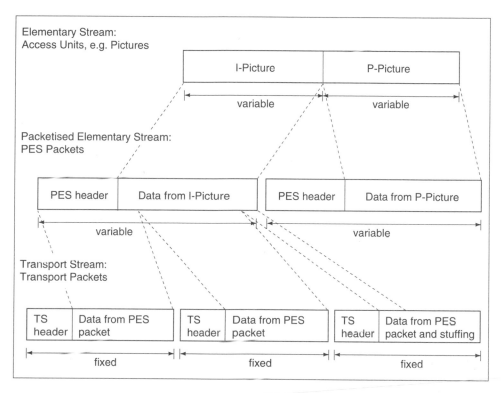

Figure 3.22: Relationship among access units,
PES packets, and transport stream packets.

data information, but all would be used with the same time base. An application for this would be a movie transmitted in different languages.

- *Multi Program Transport Streams (MPTS):* The multi program transport stream is a multiplex of a number of single program transport streams.

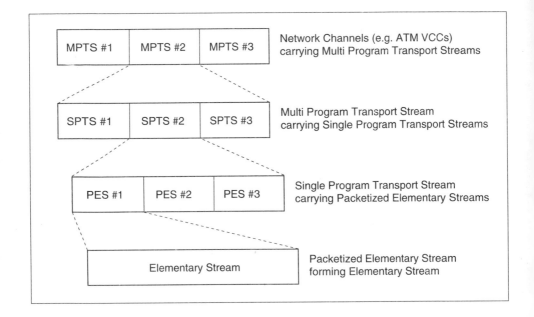

Figure 3.23: MPEG-2 System's hierarchy.

Based on the different transport stream variants, the MPEG-2 System's hierarchy is shown in Fig. 3.23.

MPEG-2 System Syntax Hierarchy

Like in MPEG-2 Video, MPEG-2 Systems use a hierarchical syntax to describe different objects. For the transport stream, this syntax hierarchy is shown in Fig. 3.24.

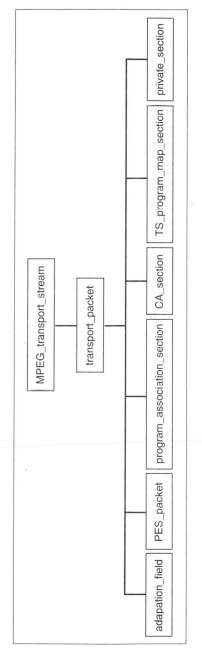

Figure 3.24: MPEG-2 System's syntax hierarchy.

Syntax Structure	Description
transport_packet	The transport packet starts with a number of indicator bits and a Packet IDentifier (PID) value. The contents of the transport packet is defined by the setting of the indicators and the value of the PID. The transport packet can contain an optional adaptation field, content data (PES-packets or private data) or program specific information (map sections).
adaptation_field	Contains timestamp information and additional information to support splicing functions.
PES_packet	The PES packet starts with a header that contains timestamp information, a stream identifier, and other indication bits. The header is followed by the actual audio and video data.
program_association_section	Table providing information about all programs in this transport stream.
CA_section	Contains information for conditional access (e.g., encryption).

Table 3.14: MPEG-2 System's high level protocol data units.

Syntax Structure	Description
TS_program_map_section	Contains information about which streams form a program.
private_section	Contains user-formatted data. This structure is used by organization such as the DVB to provide additional information, for instance, about the actual delivered service.

Table 3.14: MPEG-2 System's high level
protocol data units, *Continued*

Since the MPEG-2 transport stream plays a very important role in the whole concept of delivering video in broadband networks, the key elements of the transport stream structures will now be explained in more detail.

The transport packet

MPEG-2 defines fixed size transport packets with a fixed length of 188 bytes. This length was chosen with ATM and AAL-1 as a possible transmission method in mind. A transport packet of 188 bytes maps exactly into the payload of four ATM cells.[7] This framing method has however been superseded by the methods described in Chapter 6.

---

[7]An ATM cell has 48 bytes of payload, but one byte of the payload is used for the overhead information of ATM Adaptation Layer 1 4 × 47 = 188).

The MPEG-2 transport packet consists of 4 bytes of header information, a variable length adaptation field and the payload, containing the PES packets. Fig. 3.25 shows the MPEG-2 transport header.

One of the most important fields in the header is the so called PID (Packet IDentifier). The PID is used to identify transport packets that carry PES data from the same elementary stream, but it also defines the type of data that is transported in the packet payload. Some PID values are predefined and have a special meaning in the context of the MPEG-2 System's standard. Table 3.15 shows some of the possible PID values. For instance, for transport packets with a PID set to 0, the transport packet payload consists of a program association table structure (this table actually belongs to the so called program specific information, as described later). Transport packets with the PID value 0x10, for instance, carry PES data coming from a audio or video elementary stream.

Besides the PID, the transport packet header contains several control fields, which are used to indicate the appearance of other fields in the header and also provide information about the payload of the transport packet. A very important field is the *adaptation field*, which is described in more detail in the next section. Table 3.16 on page 113 gives a brief description of all the header fields.

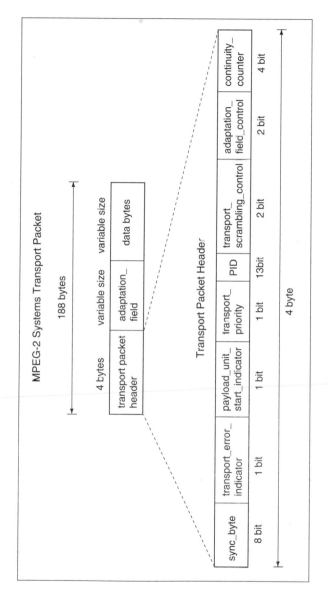

Figure 3.25: Transport packet header.

111

PID value	Description
0x0000	Program Association Table
0x0001	Conditional Access Table
0x0002-0x000F	Reserved
0x00010 to 0x1FFE	Available for PES streams, map tables, network tables
0x1FFF	Null packet

Table 3.15: Defined transport stream PIDs.

The Adaptation Field

The adaptation field is an optional field in the transport stream packet header, which contains additional information that is used for clock recovery and splicing functions. Although the data that it contains is very important for the processing of the MPEG transport stream, it is not required to have the data associated with every transport packet. Because of this, the field was made optional and is used on demand in the transport packets. One of the most important fields in the adaptation field is the program_clock_reference (PCR) field. The PCR field contains timestamp information that is used by the decoder to synchronize its clock to the encoder clock In Section 3.5.4, this concept will be explained in more detail. Beside the timestamp information, the adaptation field also has a section to transport private data, which is not defined by the MPEG-2 standard. Fig. 3.26 shows the adaptation field structure in a simplified way and Table 3.17 describes the different fields.

112

Transport Packet Header Field	Description
sync byte	The sync byte has a value of 47 (hexadecimal) and is used to identify the start of a transport packet.
transport_error_indicator	Indicates a bit error in this transport packet.
payload_unit_start_indicator	Indicates that the first byte of the transport packet payload is the start of a payload unit (e.g., a PES packet or PSI table, as explained later).
transport_priority	Can be used to indicate relative priority of transport packets.
PID	Packet Identifier (is described in detail above).
transport_scrambling_control	Indicates the scrambling used for the payload of the packet.
adaptation_field_control	Indicates if the header is followed by an adaptation field and/or payload.
continuity_counter	A counter that is incremented for each transport packet with the same PID, which contains payload. It wraps to 0 after it reaches its maximum value. This counter can be used to determine packet loss.

Table 3.16: Transport packet header fields.

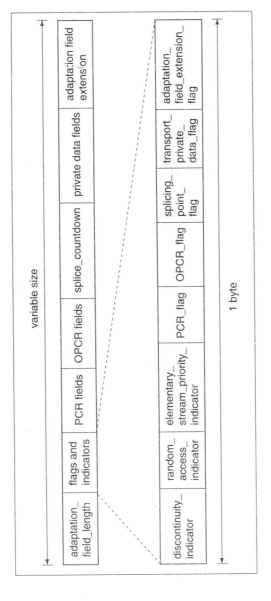

Figure 3.26: Adaptation field header.

As shown in Fig. 3.26, the adaptation field contains a number of flags and indicators at the beginning of the structure. The flags determine the remaining structure of the adaptation field. For example, if the PCR_flag was set to 1, a number of PCR related fields would be present in the adaptation field. The indication bits are used to give information about the payload. For instance, the elementary_ stream_priority bit can be set if the payload contains very important data (like an I-picture, in the case of video).

Adaptation Field Structure	Description
adapation_field_length	Contains the length of the adaptation field.
PCR fields	Contain the Program Clock Reference.
OPCR fields	Contain the original Program Clock Reference.
splice_countdown	Is used to support splicing functions.
private_data fields	Consist of a length field and the actual private data bytes. The format of the data is user definable.
adaptation field extension	Provides more information to support splicing and multiplexing of transport streams.

Table 3.17: Adaptation Field Fields

Splicing of Transport Streams

The adaptation field and the adaptation field extension contain syntax elements to support the concatenation of two different PES stream. An example of concatenation could be the insertion of a "news flash" program into a current program. If two PES streams should be concatenated, it would require knowledge of where a video or an audio access unit starts or ends. Otherwise, parts of different access units would be mixed up, which would lead to noticeable effects in the audio or video presentation. However, this requirement would mean that the MPEG-2 transport stream multiplexer would have to decode PES packets plus the audio and video access units, which is quite a complex process.

To avoid the decoding of PES packets and the transported access units, splicing points are supported by syntax elements in the adaptation field and the adaptation field extension. The splicing points give indications where in the current transport stream, a new program can be inserted. For instance, if the splice_countdown field in a transport packet reaches the value 0, it indicates that the last byte of the current transport packet payload is also the last byte of an audio or video access unit. At this point a new video or audio access unit could be inserted into the current PES stream.

The PES Packet

The PES packets are variable sized packets with a variable format. A simplified video PES packet is shown in Fig. 3.27.

The format of the PES packet is defined by a field at the very beginning of the PES packet by the *stream_id*. Table 3.18 lists some of the stream ID values defined by MPEG-2 and the meaning:

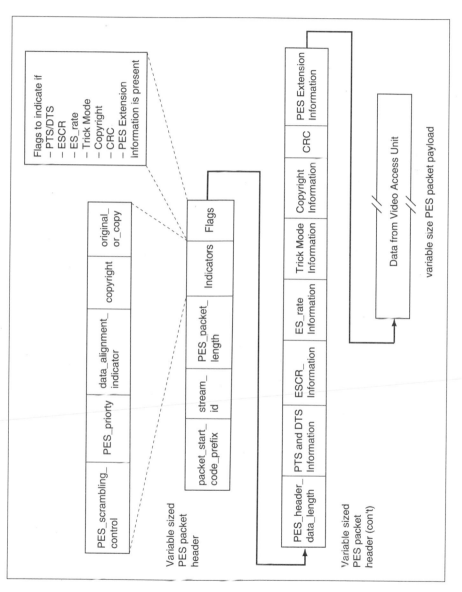

Figure 3.27: Simplified Video PES packet.

Stream ID	Stream Description
110x xxxx	MPEG-2 Audio stream number x xxxx, containing audio access units
1110 yyyy	MPEG-2 Video stream number yyyy, containing video access units
1111 0010	MPEG-2 DSM-CC stream, containing DSM-CC protocol data.

Table 3.18: PES Stream IDs.

The stream ID is followed by indicators and flags. The flags are used to further define the format of the current PES packets; the indicators are used to give additional information about the content of the PES packets. Table 3.19 shows the indicators and controls that are present in a video or audio PES packet.

The flags that might be set in the PES packet header are defining if the following information is present in the bitstream:

- Presentation Time Stamp (PTS) and Decode Time Stamp (DTS) Information: In the case of an audio or video stream, the PES packet might contain timestamp information to indicate when data should be decoded and presented. The DTS is fully optional and is only used if the decoding time of the access unit differs from the actual presentation time. However, a DTS always occurs with a related PTS. Please see Section 3.5.4 for more information about the clock values used in MPEG-2 Systems.

Indicator	Description
PES_scrambling_control	Defines if the payload is scrambled, and if yes, which user defined scrambling is used.
PES_priority	Can be set to indicate a higher priority of the current PES packet
data_alignment_indicator	Indicates that the payload starts with a video or audio start code
copyright	Indicates that the payload is copyright protected
original_or_copy	Indicates if the payload is the original or a copy

Table 3.19: PES packet header indicators.

- ESCR and ES_rate Information: The elementary stream Clock Reference (ESCR) and the Elementary Stream rate information fields are providing timing support information for the decoder. If the elementary stream is not embedded in a transport stream, this information can be used similar to the way the clock reference in the transport packet adaptation field is used.

- Trick Mode Information: The trick mode field indicates that the PES payload is representing a special (video) stream. For instance, a trick_mode_control field can be set to a value that is defined as "fast-forward," when a fast forward function is started in a interactive video on demand

(IVoD) application. There are similar settings for slow-motion, fast or slow reverse, or freeze picture.

- Copyright Information: If this bit is set to 1, the data in the PES packet is copyright protected. This information could be used to implement a simple copy protection. For example, certain operations (like storing data to disk) could be disabled after the copyright bit is checked.

- CRC Information: The PES packet can contain a CRC value, which is calculated over the PES payload of the previous PES packet.

- PES Extension Information: The PES extension is containing various fields to support buffer handling and to support MPEG-1 system streams.

3.5.3 Program Specific Information

Beside the actual video and audio information streams, the MPEG-2 transport system also carries control and management information. This information is used to group different audio and video streams together in programs. According to the MPEG-2 System's standard, a program is defined as a number of elementary streams that share a common time base. Information about this time base therefore has to be periodically transmitted by the MPEG-2 transport stream. An example for a program could be a video stream, which is combined with two audio streams and a private data stream. The two audio streams could be used to support different languages and the private data stream could contain subtitle information.

All the information structures related to the control and management of programs are grouped together in *Program Specific Information*. Program Specific Information (PSI) is basically a set of tables that are linked together. There are four tables defined by MPEG-2 Systems, forming the PSI:

- *Program Association Table (PAT)*
- *Program Map Table (PMT)*
- *Network Information Table (NIT)*
- *Conditional Access Table (CAT)*

The starting point in a multi-program transport stream is the program association table. It can be found in transport packets with the PID value 0 and provides the initial information about which programs are transported in the transport stream. For every program in the transport stream, the program association table contains an entry with a program number and a corresponding PID value. This PID value identifies those transport packets that carry another table the program map table. In Fig. 3.28 on page 124, the PAT indicates that for program #15, the program map table is found in transport packets with a PID value of 200.

The program map table provides a field called *elementary_PID*. This field contains the PID of those transport packets, carrying PES packets for a specific program. In Fig. 3.28 on page 124, the video PES packets for program #15 would be found in transport packets with the PID 500. The corresponding audio packets for this program would be in transport packets with PID values of 510 and 520. Another field in the program map table (the stream_type) defines the type of the PES

121

stream found in the transport packets identified by the elementary_PID field. For instance, the value 0x01 would indicate a MPEG-1 video stream, 0x02 would be used for an MPEG-2 Video stream, and 0x06 would indicate private data. A standard program might only use two different PIDs, one for the video and one for the audio information. However, different languages could be coded individually into separate audio streams and also text display could be implemented. The program map table also contains so called *stream descriptors,* which are used to give additional information related to the streams belonging to the program. For instance, a *video descriptor* can provide information about the chromiance sampling ratio, the profile@level combination or the frame rate, which are used for the video elementary stream. Table 3.20 shows the video related stream descriptors that are defined by MPEG-2 Systems.

In the PAT, the program #0 has a special meaning. The PID associated with program #0 is identifying those packets carrying the network information table. The network information table, carries information about the delivery network, which is used to deliver the transport stream. MPEG-2 does not define the content of the network information table and leaves this up to a network provider.

The last PSI structure that is mentioned above is the conditional access table. This table contains information about encryption methods used for video or audio data. It also contains entries for the PIDs, which identify the packets carrying control information for scrambling systems. The conditional access table is transported into transport packets with the PID value 1. Fig. 3.28 shows the relationship between the PSI tables.

Stream Descriptor	Description
video_stream_descriptor	Provides information about the coded video stream (e.g., frame rate, profile@level information, and chroma format
hierachy_descriptor	Provides information to support video scalability.
data_stream_alignment_descriptor	Indicates which video object is aligned with the start of PES packet payload (e.g., a slice, a video access unit, a group of picture, or a video sequence
target_background_grid_descriptor, video_window_descriptor	Can be used to position the decoded picture on the screen, if the picture is not occupying the complete screen.

Table 3.20: Video related stream descriptors.

PSI Table Sections

PSI table information can be segmented into sections, which are then mapped into the MPEG-2 transport packets. There are different section syntax structures to support the PAT, PMT, CAT, and private data tables. The header of the section syntax structure provides fields to indicate the section type, the section length, the actual section number,

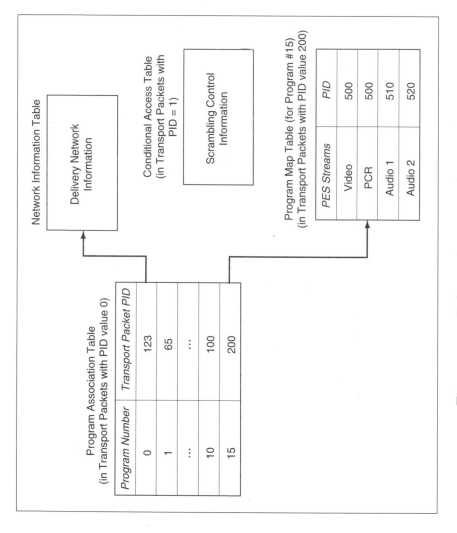

Figure 3.28: Relation between PSI Tables

and the total number of sections building the PSI table. For the private data section, the section number and total number section fields are optional. Fig. 3.29 shows the segmentation of the PMT information into sections and the mapping of the sections into transport packets. No gaps between consecutive sections are allowed and the last transport packet is filled with stuffing bytes.

3.5.4 The Program Clock Reference

The above sections described how audio and video data are transported in MPEG-2 transport streams. During the decoding process, an MPEG-2 decoder collects all MPEG-2 transport packets with the same PID and constructs/reassembles the access units. At this point, the video or audio data is not yet decoded, neither is it presented to the user. The time when the access units should be actually decoded and presented to the user is supported by the previously mentioned decode (DTS) and presentation (PTS) timestamps.

The decoder therefore needs an internal clock that can be used to determine when the exact decode or presentation time has arrived. This clock has to be very accurately synchronized with the clock that was used when the presentation and decode timestamps were created. For MPEG-2 transport streams, this clock is called the program clock and can be used for one or more programs in the MPEG-2 transport streams. To ensure that the program clock in the decoder is synchronized with the clock used for encoding/multiplexing the program, a PCR timestamp is periodically transmitted.

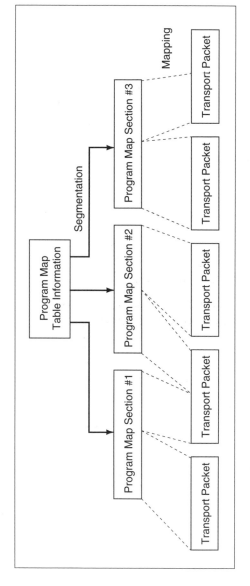

Figure 3.29: PSI section mapping in the case of a PMT

A frequency of 27 MHz was chosen for the PCR in order to be compatible with the sampling rate of CCIR-601, which is 13.5 MHz for PAL and NTSC systems. A frequency of 27 MHz implies an increment of the clock every 37 ns, which leads to a 42 bit counter in order to cover 24 hours of a day.

The PCR is transported in two parts in the adaptation field of the transport packet header, namely the program_clock_reference_base and the program_clock_reference_extension. The two parts represent two counters, running at 90 KHz and 27 MHz. As soon as the 27 MHz counter reaches the value 300, it is reset to 0 and the 90 KHz part is incremented by one. The reason for having the PCR field split into two parts is due to the fact that MPEG-1 was only using a 90 KHz timebase. In order to stay compatible here, the 27 MHz part was realized with an extension field. Another reason to treat the PCR in this special way is the format of the decode and presentation timestamps. They are also using the system clock as a reference. However, they are only 33 bit wide and can be compared easily with the value of the PCR base field. Fig. 3.30 shows the PCR fields.

To ensure that accurate timing information is always present in the system, MPEG-2 Systems specify some restrictions on the coding frequency of the different timestamp information. Table 3.21 shows the values.

The program map table for a program defines in which transport packets the PCR timestamps for this program are found by specifying the PID values of these transport packets. The system time clock in the decoder is initialized by the first transmitted PCR. When the next timestamp arrives (at least in 0.1 second intervals) the decoder's clock current time should be exactly the value of this timestamp. If not, the decoder clock has to be adjusted based on the difference between the

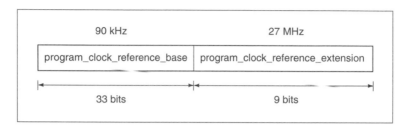

Figure 3.30: PCR fields in transport packet adaptation field

internal clock and the PCR value. The concept of using a network to transmit a resynchronization timestamp introduces some problems. It assumes that there is a constant transmission delay between the transmitting side and decoding side. If there is variation in the delay (jitter), the decoder clock could be affected.

Fig. 3.31 illustrates the PCR transmission. The decoder receives the PCR timestamp #1 and initializes its internal clock. The decoder clock then runs with an offset to the encoder clock, which corresponds to the transmission delay T. The PCR timestamp #2 is then transmitted at the time $1 + N$. If the transmission delay is constant and the decoder clock is running at the same frequency as the encoders clock,

Timestamp	transmitted at least every:
Program Clock Reference (PCR)	0,1 second
Presentation Timestamp (PTS)	0,7 second
Decode Timestamp (DTS)	optional

Table 3.21: Transmission frequency of MPEG-2 Systems timestamps.

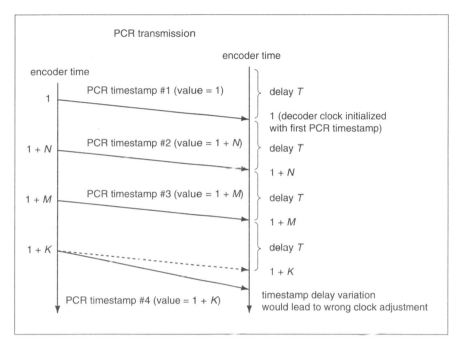

PCR transmission

encoder time

encoder time

PCR timestamp #1 (value = 1)

1

delay *T*

1 (decoder clock initialized with first PCR timestamp)

1 + *N*

PCR timestamp #2 (value = 1 + *N*)

delay *T*

1 + *N*

1 + *M*

PCR timestamp #3 (value = 1 + *M*)

delay *T*

1 + *M*

1 + *K*

delay *T*

1 + *K*

PCR timestamp #4 (value = 1 + *K*)

timestamp delay variation would lead to wrong clock adjustment

Figure 3.31: PCR transmission.

this PCR is then received at the decoders time $1 + N$. After some time, the PCR timestamp #3 is transmitted at the time $1 + M$. Again, if the delay is constant and the clocks are running with the same frequency, the value for $1 + M$, transmitted from the encoder, and the $1 + M$ in the decoder should be the same. If there would be a difference and the delay would be assumed as constant, the decoder clock variance would have to be adjusted.

The PCR timestamp #4 is transmitted with a value of $1 + K$ and is delayed. Assuming again that the encoder and decoder clocks are running with the same frequency (K in the encoder equals K in the decoder), the received PCR timestamp would incorrectly indicate that the decoder clock needs to be adjusted.

This problem is specifically important if the MPEG-2 data is transported over jitter-introducing networks (e.g., B-ISDN based on ATM). In B-ISDN there are a few approaches to encounter this problem. One example is the use of a constant bit rate emulation on top of the ATM technology. This emulation is realized with the ATM adaptation layer type 1, which is explained in more detail in Chapter 4.

Even if the underlying network services would always be provided with a constant delay, delay can be introduced by processing of the MPEG-2 layer itself. MPEG-2 transport stream multiplexers, which influence the MPEG-2 Systems layer directly, are therefore adjusting the PCR values according to the delay they are introducing.

3.5.5 Error Detection in MPEG-2 Systems

The MPEG-2 System's part also provides functionality to detect errors in the transport stream. Most of the error detection is done with parts of the transport stream packet header, as seen in Fig. 3.32.

- Transport error indication bit: This bit can be set by the MPEG-2 equipment (e.g., by a MPEG-2 transport stream multiplexer) to show that this transport packet has an error in the header or the payload. When a transport packet that is tagged with this bit is received by the decoding

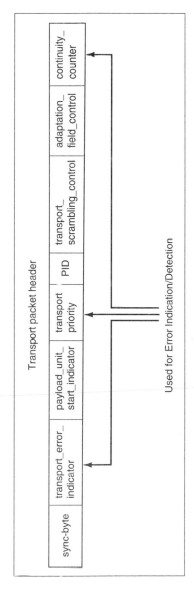

Figure 3.32: Bits to use for error indication and prevention.

unit, the decoder could take the necessary actions to decode the packet with additional error concealment mechanisms. This could also indicate that the quality level of the network services would have to be increased.

- Transport priority bit: With this bit set, the transport packet is tagged as a high priority packet. It should receive high priority treatment in the case of congestion conditions in a network, where data needs to be discarded. An application might be to tag those transport packets that carry the video_sequence_header information as a high priority packet. Since network protocols like ATM have similar priority bits defined, a relation between MPEG-2 transport packet priority and the network priority is possible.

- Continuity Counter bits: The value in those four bits is incremented for each transport packet with the same PID. With this kind of counter packet loss, events are easy to detect.

- Elementary Stream priority bit: Similar to Transport priority bit, but on the PES packet level (see Fig. 3.27 on page 117).

Beside those indication bits, MPEG-2 also uses CRC checksums in different places to protect the transported information. The PES packet header can contain an optional field, which is used to transmitted a CRC value calculated over the data bytes of the previous PES packet. CRC values are also used for each of the PSI tables.

3.6 MPEG-2 Digital Storage Medium— Command and Control (DSM-CC)

3.6.1 Introduction

Beside dealing with the video and audio aspects of digital video systems, the MPEG standardization group is also working on more network related subjects. With the design and architecture of multimedia services in mind, it quickly turned out that a standard had to be created to control the information flow between the video source and the receiving equipment. This work has been started by the DSM-CC group.

The DSM-CC protocols supplement other networking protocols, like B-ISDN signaling or transport protocols, in order to cover all requirements of video networks. DSM-CC signaling assumes that the network links between the different entities are already established. This can be done manually, for instance, by using network management and configuration tools, or it could be done with network signaling protocols, like the ones defined for B-ISDN and ATM (see Section 4). Fig. 3.33 shows the DSM-CC protocol in relation to other protocols in a video on demand system.

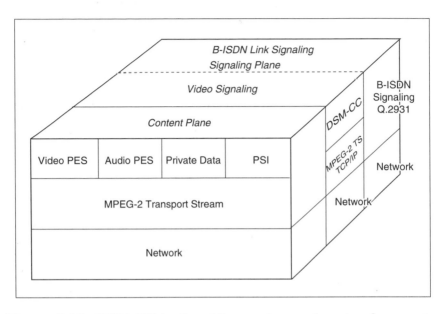

Figure 3.33: DSM-CC in the video on demand protocol scenario.

After an initial link has been set up between the two entities in the video delivery network, DSM-CC provides the functionality to continue the setup of a application session. Because this session set up happens at the interface between network and user equipment, DSM-CC defines a DSM-CC user to network protocol. Once the application session has been setup, further logical links are established between a video server and a set top box. One logical link might be used for user data (like MPEG-2 coded video) and another logical link might be used to control what is happening on the user data link (see Fig. 3.34).

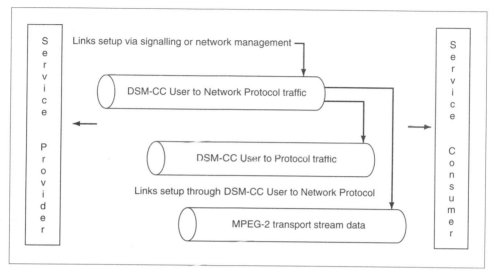

Figure 3.34: Links between server and client.

The actual protocol to be used on this control link is not specified by DSM-CC. However, DSM-CC defines a set of services (e.g., to manipulate a video stream) in the server, which can be used by the client. Because these services are only relevant between two user entities (e.g., the server and the client), the DSM-CC standard refers to them as the DSM-CC user-to-user interface.

These two DSM-CC interfaces are fundamentally different. The user-network interface has much in common with OSI Layer 3 signaling protocols, like PDU structures and procedures for session setup and tear-down. The user–user part of DSM-CC is application layer oriented, and, as we will see later, uses an object oriented approach. Fig. 3.35 illustrates the two different interfaces DSM-CC addresses.

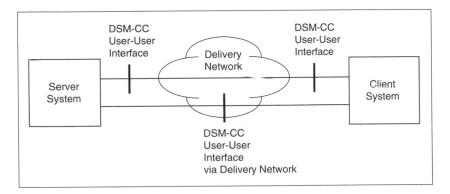

Figure 3.35: DSM-CC User-to-Network and User-to-User interfaces.

3.6.2 User-to-Network Operations

The user–network operations mainly focus on the management and control of sessions between the user equipment and the network. User equipment can be either the video server or the client (e.g., a set top box).

To support user-network operations, DSM-CC defines messages and command sequences. A DSM-CC user-network message always consists of a message header and the message payload. The message header contains several important fields like DSM-CC message type, messageId and transactionId. The message header is shown in Fig. 3.36 and the fields belonging to it are briefly described in Table 3.22.

The format of the message payload depends on the actual messageId and on the DSM-CC messagetype. DSM-CC distinguishes between two groups of messages at the user-to-network interface:

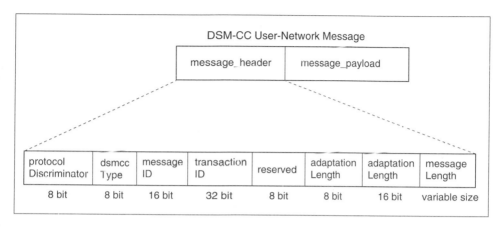

Figure 3.36: DSM-CC message header.

- User-to-Network Configuration Messages: Configuration message are used to transmit DSM-CC specufic, network specific, or even user definable configuration parameters between user equipment and network. These parameters can include timer and counter values for the DSM-CC session and resource management protocol, as well as network parameters like client or server addresses. Table 3.23 on page 140 lists the currently defined user–network configuration messages.

- User-to-Network (Session and Resource Management) Messages: This group of messages is used to setup and manage video application sessions. It forms a very essential part of the DSM-CC standard and is explained in detail in the section on User-to-Network Message.

Header Field	Description
protocol Discriminator	Identifies this message as a DSM-CC message.
dsmccType	Identifies the type of the DSM-CC message, (e.g., the message could be a user–to–network configuration message, a user–to–network message, a user–to–user configuration message, or user–to–user message
messageId	Consists of three parts : • messageDescriminator, indicating if the message is passed between client and network or server and network • message scenario, describing the scenario in which the message is currently used (e.g., during session set up or session tear-down) • messageType, indicating if the user or the network is sending the message and if the message exchange is initiated by the user or the network. messageType can be: ▪ Request: Sent from the user to the network

Table 3.22: DSM-CC message header fields.

Header Field	Description
	▪ Confirm: Sent from network to user in reply to Request - Indication: Sent from network to user ▪ Response: Sent from the user to the network in reply to indication Based on these components, DSM-CC is defining messages, which are listed in Fig. 3.39.
transactionId	Is a unique identifier to support the message processing
adaptationLength	Gives the length of the optional dsmcc Adaptation Header
messageLength	Gives the length of message
dsmccAdaptationHeader	On optional header field to support conditional access or user defined information

Table 3.22: DSM-CC message header fields.

Message Name	Description
UNConfigRequest	Sent from user to network to request configuration from the network
UNConfigConfirm	Sent from network to the user in response to a UNConfigRequest
UNConfigIndication	Sent from network to the user to configure a User device
UNConfigResponse	Sent from the user to the network in response to a UNConfigIndication

Table 3.23: DSM-CC configuration messages.

3.6.2 User-to-Network Messages

A user-to-network message consists of the message header and the message payload. The message payload consists of data fields, a number of optional resource descriptors, and user definable data bytes. Data fields are typically defined as a fixed number of bytes, containing a single value like a counter, an identifier, or a reason code.

The resource descriptors are more complex objects based on a common resource descriptor structure. Different resource descriptors are identified by a type field in this structure. Fig. 3.37 shows the currently defined data fields and resource descriptors.

Data fields carry more general information like session identifier, client identifiers or reason codes. The session identifier, for example, is a very important field in the DSM-CC user-to-network message. Server and client implementations can use the session identifier to keep track of

140

Field Name	Resource Descriptors
cfSessionId	ContinuousFeedSession
clientId	AtmConnection
deviceId	MpegProgram
reason	PhysicalChannel
response	TSUpstreamBandwidth
resourceCount	TSDownStreamBandwidth
serverId	AmtSvcConnection
sessionId	AtmConnectionNotify
sessionNum	IP
statusByte	ClientTDMAAssignment
statusCount	SharedResources
statusType	SharedRequestId
userId	UserDefined
	TypeOwner

Figure 3.37: Data fields and resource descriptors in DSM-CC.

resources belonging to a session by assigning the session identifier to them. If the session is released later, the resources identified by the session identifier can be released as well. Also, the session identifier is used if certain resources should be added to or removed from a specific session.

A resource descriptor carries resource related information (e.g., the bandwidth to be used for video data). The resource data is therefore very much related to the underlying delivery network and the transported MPEG-2 data elements. Resource data is always related to a specific session. As an example the resource descriptor "Atm Connection" uses the resource fields shown in Table 3.24.

Resource field	Description
atmAddress	The ATM address of the client/ server.
atmVci	The ATM VCI value used for the session. (See chapter 4).
atmVpi	The ATM VPI value used for the session. (See chapter 4)

Table 3.24: DSM-CC user-to-network resource: ATMConnection.

With all of the above mentioned payload elements, data fields and resources descriptors, the DSM-CC standard then defines the actual user-to-network messages. Fig. 3.38 summarizes the building blocks of a DSM-CC User-Network message.

DSM-CC defines messages for the communication between the client and the network and also messages for communication between the server and the network. Fig. 3.39 shows the most important user-to-network messages:

The above listed messages are then used in command sequences. The command sequences can be separated into three groups: 1) client initiated command sequences, 2) server initiated command sequences, and 3) network initiated command sequences.

- **Client Initiated command sequences**
  An example for a client initiated command sequence is the session setup command sequence. The command sequence is processed when a client (e.g., a set top box) goes on-line

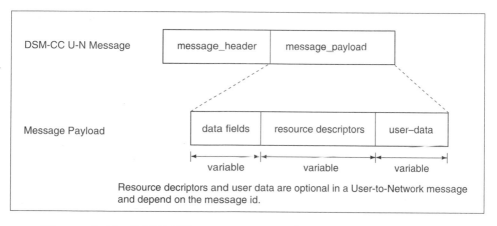

Figure 3.38: DSM-CC user-to-network message components.

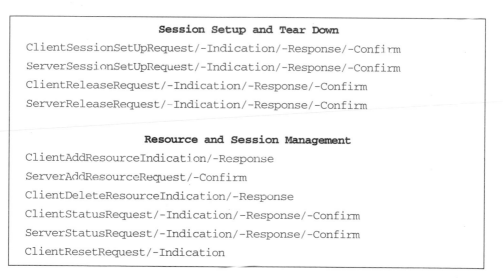

Figure 3.39: DSM-CC user-to-network messages.

(is switched on) and an application session has to be established with the server. Fig. 3.40 shows a simplified message flow for this command sequence.

Besides this command sequence, other client initiated command sequences are defined:

- Release of a session: The session release command sequence is processed when the user leaves the application and the previously assigned resources can be freed up.

- Status request command sequence: A client can send a status request message to get information about the currently active sessions, the configuration that is used for a session, and the status of a specific session.

- **Server initiated command sequences**
  An example for a server initiated command sequence is the continuous feed session set-up command sequence, where a program is broadcast to a number of clients. Other server initiated command sequences are:

  - Session setup command sequence: Some applications require that a session is set-up from the server side. Examples of this would be tele-learning applications or special broadcasts, where central control is implemented.

  - Session resource reprovision, add resources command sequences: These command sequences are executed if, for some reason, the assigned resources have to be modified or new resources have to be added to the session. An example would be an application that would require an additional logical data channel between server and set top box (e.g., to support the data download).

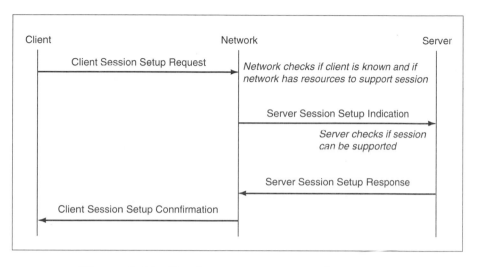

Figure 3.40: Session setup command sequence.

- Session release, continuous feed session release command sequences: Sometimes the server needs to tear down a session, for instance, to perform system maintenance.

- **Network initiated command sequences**
  Network initiated command sequences are mainly session tear-down sequences, if, for some reason, the network is not able to provide the requested network service any longer. Besides the session tear-down sequences, the network also polls the user equipment by client or server status requests. The result of the polling sequence could lead to a network initiated session tear-down of the session between server and network, if the client no longer responds to the status request. Network initiated command sequences are:

- Session release, Continuous feed session release
- Client status request, Server status request

3.6.3 User-to-User Operations

The previously described DSM-CC user to network functionality, is used to set-up and tear-down video application sessions, or manage the resources needed for the session. However, as stated at the beginning of this chapter, DSM-CC also deals with end-to-end communication between server and client. This kind of communication is transparent to the network and is therefore defined as *user-to-user* operations. User-to-user operations can be grouped into two parts: application download communication and client-server communication.

Application Download Communication

The application download operations are primarily used for loading executable code from the server to a client. In a service on demand scenario, this could, for instance, be a navigator application software, which is downloaded right after the session between the server and client is set-up. For standard download communication, DSM-CC defines a simple message-based protocol, which also implements a basic data flow-control mechanism. Besides this flow-control-based, point-to-point download protocol, DSM-CC foresees the use of a broadcasting approach for download purposes. To support broadcast download, DSM-CC introduces the idea of a data carousel, where download data is continuously provided on a well defined download channel. Clients can tune to this channel, identify the data that is provided for download by analyzing periodically transmitted download control messages, and finally capture the data they are interested in.

Client-Server Communication

After a session has been set-up between the client and the server, the actual software application implementing the service can be started. This software typically consists of two components, one being executed on the client (set top unit or PC) side and another on the server side. Both components communicate with each other to perform different tasks. The client software on the PC or set top unit typically provides some kind of user interface, allowing the user to navigate and use the actual service. In the server software, requests from the user are processed (e.g., a movie is started).

This communication is very much application oriented and is mostly transparent to the network. For instance, to realize VCR functionality in an Interactive Video on Demand application, commands like fast-forward, rewind or pause have to be transmitted from the client to server. Those commands can be implemented by using the user-to-user part of the DSM-CC.

Interactive video services are basically distributed client-server applications, which can be realized in different ways. The computer industry established the so called *Object Management Group (OMG)*, in order to define a common, object-oriented architecture *(CORBA)* to support distributed applications. It would go far beyond the scope of this book to go into much detail with this object-oriented architecture. Fundamentally though, this architecture helps to define interfaces that are used to access functions and services implemented by distributed objects. The interfaces are described by using a *Interface Definition Language (IDL)*.[8]

DSM-CC user-user uses the CORBA concept heavily to define interfaces to different functions, which are assumed to be provided by a server system. However, the compatibility with CORBA makes DSM-CC user-to-user attractive and unattractive at the same time. On the one hand, it is, of course, a big benefit to support a widely supported distributed computing platform. It should make it quite easy to include video service components into bigger software application systems. However, on the other hand, CORBA does currently imply very heavy system performance requirements (both in terms of memory and processing power required). This sets some constraints regarding the hardware to be used to implement the application. A classic example for a situation where these constraints are an issue is the low-cost set-top box where memory and processing resources are very limited.

But let's come back to the example of the interactive video on demand application. DSM-CC user-user defines, for example, the functions for the (video) stream manipulation interface, as seen in Table 3.25.

Fig. 3.41 shows the IDL definition for the DSM Stream Play function. Three input parameters are defined, the start (rStart) and the stop (rStop) time, as well as the scale (rScale), which defines the speed and the play direction (forward/backward) for this stream.

---

[8]If an application needs to use one of the functions, it does not need to know about the location of the object that implements the function. It requests the function and the Object Request Broker (ORB) resolves the location of the object, triggers the execution of the function, and delivers the result back to the calling application.

Function	Description
DSM Stream Pause	Stop sending stream when a specific position is reached.
DSM Stream Resume	Start sending stream at a specific position.
DSM Stream Status	Obtain the status of stream.
DSM Stream Reset	Reset the stream state machine.
DSM Stream Jump	Jump to a specific position in the stream, if a certain position is reached.
DSM Stream Play	Play a stream from position A to position B.

Table 3.25: DSM-CC user-to-user function
for stream manipulation interface.

Beside the stream interface, DSM-CC user-to-user defines the following other core interfaces:

- Base and Access Interface: This interface defines operations and attributes which are used by other interfaces.

- Directory interface: The Directory interface implements a name service in order to access and find DSM-CC User-to-User objects by names.

- File interface: The file interface provides simple file operations like read and write. For instance the client can save a personal user profiles on the server.

```
Client-Service IDL Syntax
module DSM {
  interface Stream : Base, Access{
      void play (
           in AppNPT rStart,
           in AppNPT rStop,
           in Scale rScale)
           raises (MPEG_DELIVERY,BAD_START,BAD_STOP,BAD_SCALE);
                     };
      };
```

Figure 3.37: Data fields and resource descriptors in DSM-CC.

- Service Gateway interface: The service gateway interfaces provides the necessary functions to allow a client to access a services.

Besides these core interfaces, DSM-CC user-to-user also defines so called extended interfaces, for instance, to allow an application to use SQL statements to query a movie database or implement security mechanisms.

3.7 To Get More Details . . .

For a complete coverage of the MPEG technology, it is recommended to get the ISO/IEC standards [29-32, 34-36]. MPEG was and still is subject to several articles in different publications. Communications Technology magazine [40] gave an introduction to MPEG-2 Systems , the IEEE Communications magazine [2] presented an very good overview about MPEG-2 DSM-CC. The FKT Magazine [25] had a series of articles about MPEG-2, covering video, audio and systems (in German). A number of seminars with MPEG as one of the main topics have been presented (e.g., the IEE Electronics Division Colloquium about MPEG-2 [41]). It is also always worthwhile to check out the MPEG web home page at http://drogo.cselt.stet.it/mpeg/ or at http://www.mpeg.org. To learn more about MPEG and other video and audio compression algorithms and the actual implementation of encoder and decoder hard- and software, Vasudev Bhaskaran's and Konstantinos Konstantinides book [33] about video and image compression standards is highly recommended. The publications from the Audio Engineering Society, as for instance [8], are recommended; they are frequently covering different aspects of audio compression. To get more details about the new client-server applications architectures and standards, the "Client-Server Survival Guide" [53] is an excellent source.

4

Broadband Network Technologies

4.1 Broadband Network Technologies—On a Page

To be able to transport the MPEG compressed digital video signals through the network, from the encoder to the set top box for instance, a very powerful transmission mechanism is needed. Presently, the only technology that can fulfill all the requirements in terms of bandwidth, flexibility, and interactivity the digital video services have is the ATM protocol, the central element of the B-ISDN. This section will provide the background and the essential technical details of B-ISDN needed to enable a more detailed understanding of the key networking technologies, referred to in the later section dealing with "Video in Broadband Networks." The following will be covered:

- The reasons for defining the B-ISDN—the history and background.

- The major interface points and network elements in the B-ISDN are defined in order to provide insight in the basic functional blocks and reference points.

- A detailed description of the organization of the different layers and protocols used in B-ISDN. The most cental aspects of these layers and protocols will then be dealt with in detail. This will cover the description of function and structure of:

  - The physical layer and the transmission convergence layer, with special focus on some of the most central protocols, DS-3, E-3 PDH, and, in particular, SONET OC-3/SDH STM-1.

  - The ATM layer, including the ATM layer Quality of Service (QoS) aspects relevant for transporting digital video over ATM.

  - The ATM adaptation layers with special focus on the protocols relevant for transporting MPEG-2 compressed digital video, AAL-1 and AAL-5, and finally the higher protocol layers with special focus on signaling, particularly the ITU protocol for UNI Signaling Q.2931.

4.2 History and Background of B-ISDN

The concept of B-ISDN was originally defined in the late 1980s. It is a collection of technologies with ATM as the "cornerstone," which is expected to form a universal network. The B-ISDN is essentially characterized by the ability to convey all present and future types of information, at very high speeds, and in a cost efficient manner. This is a contrast to the present situation, where a multitude of different networks coexist to provide services of different kinds. The present structure, where the telephone network can transfer voice and data at low speeds, the X.25, or Frame Relay connection, which can transfer data at medium speeds, and broadcasting or cable TV, which can convey television, presents an inefficient use of resources. This is due to the fact that each and all of these networks must be installed and maintained separately. Furthermore, when resources become available on one network, for instance, on the telephone network in the time interval after the 9–5 business peak hours, these resources cannot be made available for other networks or services, such as television.

An effort to cope with these drawbacks of the existing telecommunication infrastructure was made with the development and implementation of the Narrowband ISDN (N-ISDN). This network can transport voice, data, and, in principle, video. The N-ISDN has some limitations, however:

- ISDN has a fairly limited bandwidth, namely 144 Kbps with the basic rate interface, and 2 Mbps with the primary rate interface. This is probably suitable for most normal

155

uses presently, but within a short time normal bandwidth requirements are likely to have risen beyond these rates. For example, a typical broadcast quality service carrying MPEG-2 compressed video, normally require at least 4 Mbps.

- N-ISDN is inflexible in many aspects. The user must for instance pay for the maximum bandwidth of the connection during a call, regardless of how much of the bandwidth capacity he actually uses.

- Only relatively few services supports the N-ISDN concept.

The next step in this evolution is B-ISDN. It has been the subject of much work, since the standardization body ITU in 1988 declared that ATM should be the basis of the future B-ISDN. Field trials have been done, and are still being done, all over the world in order to give telecom operators and equipment manufactures practical experience with B-ISDN. Presently, field trials involving B-ISDN networks with MPEG-2 compressed digital video services are done. The most important parts of B-ISDN, such as like ATM and SDH, have been finalized. Some standards may, however, still need to be developed further and refined, in order to enable a fully working B-ISDN that can cope with the multitude of potential new services.

4.3 Abilities and Benefits of B-ISDN

4.3.1 Introduction

There are a number of advantages of B-ISDN compared with the existing network structures. Some of the most important are the following six:

- Application independence
- Bandwidth efficiency
- LAN-MAN-WAN integration
- Bandwidth granularity
- Dynamic bandwidth
- Variable connection quality

It is mainly due to these qualities that ATM and B-ISDN have received so much attention in the tele/datacommunication business over the last years, and now also in the video business. The details of these six overall advantage areas will here be dealt with in more detail.

4.3.2 Application Independence

With the B-ISDN, only one network is needed to cover all the different possible services. It can convey information of different kinds, with different characteristics, namely:

- Data: Constant or variable bit rate data. Data transfer, such as LAN connections, often comes with bursts of traffic in short periods—typically in the range of milliseconds. Data transfer is normally not sensitive to delay in the network, unless real-time applications are involved. (Small delays in a file transfer is of no importance, for instance.) The bandwidth requirements of a data transfer is normally from 64 Kbps to 10 Mbps, but in principle there is no limit. Presently, 155 Mbps and even 622 Mbps connections to the desk top are being developed and commercially deployed.

- Video: Video or television transmission, including everything from the relatively low VHS quality (or lower), all the way over HDTV quality to studio quality, is sensitive to delay, and especially to delay variation. It has constant (or in some cases varying) bandwidth demand of typically 180—270 Mbps in uncompressed format. (e.g., MPEG-2), the bandwidth requirements typically lie in the range from 1.5—80 Mbps. The burstiness of variable bite rate video is normally lower than in the case of, let's say, data transfer connections.

- Voice: A constant 64 Kbps bandwidth requirement characterizes voice transfer from telephones, as we know it today. The transfer of voice is highly delay sensitive, since even small delays or interrupts are perceived to be annoying by the human ear. Longer delays can make communication virtually impossible.

- Combinations of the above mentioned or multimedia applications, which could, for instance, be interactive TV, such as tele-shopping, tele-education, or transmission of other

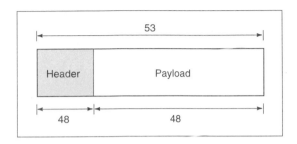

Figure 4.1: Structure of the ATM cell.

multimedia services, including text, images, sound, video, and possibly other types of information.

The fact that one network can convey all these different types of information, with different demands to bandwidth, burstiness, etc., is primarily due to ATM technology. It conveys information in small "cells" or packets of 53 bytes, 48 bytes for user information and 5 header bytes for different control purposes, as shown in Fig. 4.1. The information coming from the different services, such as file transfers or video transmissions, are segmented to fit into the ATM cell by the so called ATM adaptation layer (explained in detail later), and multiplexed into one stream of ATM cells.

The information flows from (or to) different users, for instance a specific type of video service can be collected in the network and transmitted via specific channels or paths, which can provide the required performance. The information of what channels or paths the information should be led via, is located in the 5 byte header of each ATM cell.

The fact that the ATM cell is of a fixed size instead of a varying size, enables simpler and much faster processing in all network components,

159

such as interface cards and switches, as processing of the cells can be done in HW rather than SW. Furthermore, it is not necessary to calculate packet length, allocate varying buffer space, etc., as variable length packets require. Finally, the ATM cell is only 53 bytes long. Hereby delay sensitive applications will not be delayed significantly from the time it takes to "fill" a cell with information.

4.3.3 Bandwidth Efficiency

In contrast to "synchronous transfer mode" or "time division multiplexing," (TDM) as it is normally called, ATM uses the bandwidth of a connection in a fairly efficient way. TDM is found in a great deal of the existing communications network, for instance, in the existing telephone network, utilizing the Plesiochronous Digital Hierarchy (PDH) technology. With TDM, the bandwidth of a given connection is shared in a fixed way among the users. Each user has a "time slot," which is available to him or her, whether it is needed or not. See Fig. 4.2. If, for instance, one user is inactive, this causes a 33 percent capacity waste.

TDM guarantees the required bandwidth with an acceptable, constant delay. But it is inefficient in its use of the transmission capacity. In ATM, the access to the network is in principle unlimited, dependent only on the capacity available. This is also referred to as "statistical multiplexing."

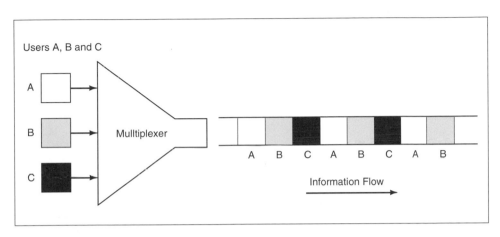

Figure 4.2: The structure of TDM.

4.3.4 LAN-MAN-WAN Integration

B-ISDN is well suited for use in LANs, MANs, and WANs. Combined with the fact that ATM is independent of the physical layer protocols and cables, ATM cells can be transported on all the networks. This drastically reduces the need for protocol conversion, as we presently when we transport LAN traffic over a WAN connection. Furthermore, the independence of the physical layer means that the installed base of wiring can be re-used.

4.3.5 Bandwidth Granularity

Today, users and network element designers have to respect the discrete "blocks" in which bandwidth is available. These blocks are normally based on multiples of 64 Kbps, such as 2, 8, or 34 Mbps. With

B-ISDN, it is the other way around. Here, the network can be tailored to closely fit to the bandwidth demands of the application, since the minimum unit of information is the 48 bytes of payload in the ATM cell. In practice, the bandwidth requirements, among other parameters, are specified at the time when the connection is established.

4.3.6 Dynamic Bandwidth

When a connection is initiated, the bandwidth requirements of the connection, in terms of traffic rate and burstiness, are "negotiated" with the network via the signaling procedures, as described later. If the demands change during the call, the connection parameters can be renegotiated. Furthermore, the user can be billed for the actual bandwidth he or she uses, if required. Expressed in a popular manner, he or she can be charged "for the number of cells used." Finally, the B-ISDN has no upper limit with respect to bandwidth. This depends primarily on the capabilities of the physical layer components at a given time. Presently, the bandwidth available to the end user is typically lying in the range of T1/E1 (1.5 or 2 Mbps), T3/E3 (45 or 34 Mbps), or the ATM Forum 25.6 Mbps. For the core network, SDH STM-1 or SONET OC-3 (155 Mbps) is used, as well as SDH STM-4 or SONET OC-12 (622 Mbps).

4.3.7 Variable Connection Quality

It is possible for the user to specify what "Quality of Service" (QoS) he wants from the network. In the B-ISDN, if, for instance, a moderate level of cell delay variation is a minor problem for the service used, this can be specified when the connection is initiated, and possibly renegotiated later as desired. In this way, it is possible for the user only to pay for what he needs, and chances are that the network is used more efficiently.

4.4 Description of Selected Network Elements and Structures

4.4.1 Introduction

This description of the network elements and structures in B-ISDN is by no means meant to be exhaustive, it should rather be seen as an introduction to the most central components. It is necessary to understand the basic functions and terms of the elements that build a B-ISDN network, as these are closely related to the different protocols that will later be described in detail.

Equipment types like switches and terminal equipment essentially perform the functions of a LEX/TEX or B-NTs and B-TEs, respectively. (In this example, the terminal equipment could be a B-ISDN compliant set top box.) To perform the functions of for instance the B-NT and B-TE, the equipment includes an implementation of a range of protocols. This could include a given physical interface complying with the SDH or PDH protocols, as well as an implementation of ATM and an ATM adaptation layer, like AAL-1 or AAL-5. The information that has been transported and protected by these protocols is then passed to the part of the equipment that handles the MPEG-2 transport stream, as well as the actual decoding. This part of the equipment is based on an implementation of the MPEG protocols. Finally, to control the whole set-up of connections through the network (in the case of VoD for instance), the equipment would also typically include an implementation of UNI signaling, as well as DSM-CC.

The following presented structure is similar in many aspects to the definitions made in N-ISDN. There is a clear distinction between the network on the customers' premises, and the public network utilizing the UNI and the NNI respectively. It should be noted that the network elements and the reference points are essentially referring to an abstract conceptual model of what functional blocks and demarcation points a B-ISDN includes. Commercially available equipment typically includes several functional blocks (like for instance B-NT and B-TE). Therefore, more demarcation points are covered in one piece of equipment, as the Sb and the Tb in this example. The definition of the network elements and the reference points serve as a practical framework when discussing B-ISDN networks. For the following, please refer to Fig. 4-3.

4.4.2 Network Elements

The following five types of network elements comprise the equipment that utilizes the so called User Network Interface (UNI). The UNI typically resides in the private part of the network (i.e., on the end users premises). Equipment in the public network (e.g., large transmission switches), use the interface generally referred to as the Network Node Interface (NNI). The UNI and NNI are different in more aspects—as described later—for instance, the ATM cell format is slightly different and the signaling protocols differ.

The broadband terminal equipment (B-TE) handles communication, performs protocol handling, connection, and maintenance functions, among other things, on the customers premises. Two types of B-TEs are defined by the ITU-T:

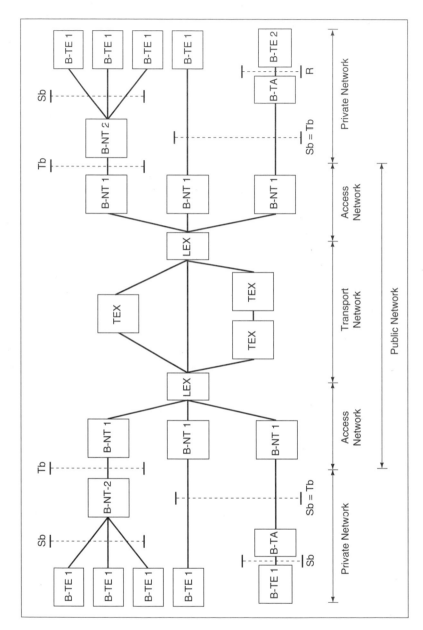

Figure 4.3: The various reference points and network elements of B-ISDN.

- B-TE 1: Performs the above mentioned functions and is equipped with a B-ISDN compliant interface. It could, for instance, be a set top box or a PC / workstation with a interface card, complying to B-ISDN standards. (i.e., it would have implemented a physical layer protocol that can carry ATM cells.)

- B-TE 2: Equivalent to B-TE 1 but with a non B-ISDN interface. This could be a PC with an RS 232 or Ethernet LAN connection, (i.e., no ATM cells are carried via the physical layer protocols). A broadband terminal adapter (B-TA) converts information to and from B-TE 2 type equipment, to protocols that comply with B-ISDN standards.

Two types of broadband network termination equipment (B-NT) are also defined:

- B-NT 1: The first type of network termination equipment has a minimum of functions that are needed by all customers. It covers a range of functions defined in the physical layer in the OSI model, namely termination of the public network, generation, and reception of maintenance cells, bit timing and cell delineation in some cases.

- B-NT 2: The second type of network termination equipment is more advanced than the first. A B-NT 2 type of equipment is needed if more than one terminal is used with the B-NT 1 connection. It can have multiplexing/demultiplexing functions, local switching capabilities (to enable that local phone calls or data transfers stay within the user network, for instance), as well as buffering capabilities for ATM cells. A LAN using ATM can be said to have B-NT 2 functionality, as well.

4.4.3 Reference Points

As can be seen in Fig. 4.3, three reference points have been defined:

- R—reference point: This is a non B-ISDN interface, such as RS 232 or X. 21, between the B-TA and non B-ISDN compliant equipment.
- Sb—reference point: This is the interface between B-NT 2 and B-TE or B-TA equipment.
- Tb—reference point: This marks the division between the customer premises and the public network, between the B-NT 1 and B-NT 2. At both the Sb and Tb reference points, all communication and interfaces are B-ISDN compliant.

4.4.4 Public Network Elements

Apart from the B-NT 1 that was described above, there are a number of other important public network elements that deserve a closer look.

- Local exchange (LEX): a LEX can interface to B-NTs on one side and other local exchanges, or transit exchanges (described later) on the other side. It may perform some or all of the following functions:

- Switching (routes ATM cells through the network)
- Call control (sets up a connection before the actual user information transfer is initiated and release the connection after use)
- Usage parameter control, UPC (monitors and takes action if a connection exceeds the resource limits allocated to it)
- Charging functions
- Transit exchange (TEX): A TEX interfaces only to other TEXs or LEXs . It has larger switching capabilities than the LEX, but there is no need for any of the other functions, such as charging functions, as these are already performed by the LEXs.

4.5 B-ISDN Protocols

4.5.1 Introduction

To be able to understand the possibilities, as well as the limitations, of transmitting services like digital video over a B-ISDN network, it is essential to understand the functionality of the involved protocols, as well as how the different protocols relate. Without this background, it is hardly possible to understand how a given quality of service can be achieved in a B-ISDN network, how connections can be established on demand to support services like video on demand, as well as why the B-ISDN is considered as probably the most powerful and flexible network existing today.

The network elements just described need to follow a predefined way of exchanging information, so that network communication protocols are implemented in the components throughout the network, like servers, switches, terminal equipment, etc.

As it is common when describing tele- or datacommunication protocols, the protocols used in B- ISDN are best illustrated by a layered model. This section will give a general understanding of the protocol model found in B-ISDN, an introduction to the functions of the different layers, as well as a more detailed understanding of the most relevant protocols.

The organization of the protocols used in B-ISDN can be illustrated by the model seen in Fig. 4.4, as well as in Fig. 4.5. These are abstract models, essentially serving the purpose of defining a common framework in terms of how the protocols are related.

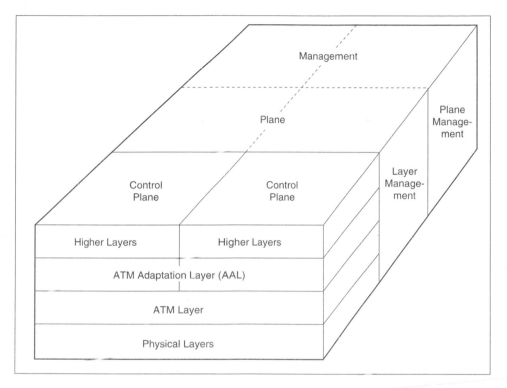

Figure 4.4: Layers and planes that comprises the B-ISDN.

The functionality of the protocols are grouped into different "planes," each with a different fundamental task. The planes are listed below:

- The *user plane* provides the actual information transfer. This is the major part of the functionality used when transmitting the actual MPEG compressed video/audio stream (or any other type of service) through the network from

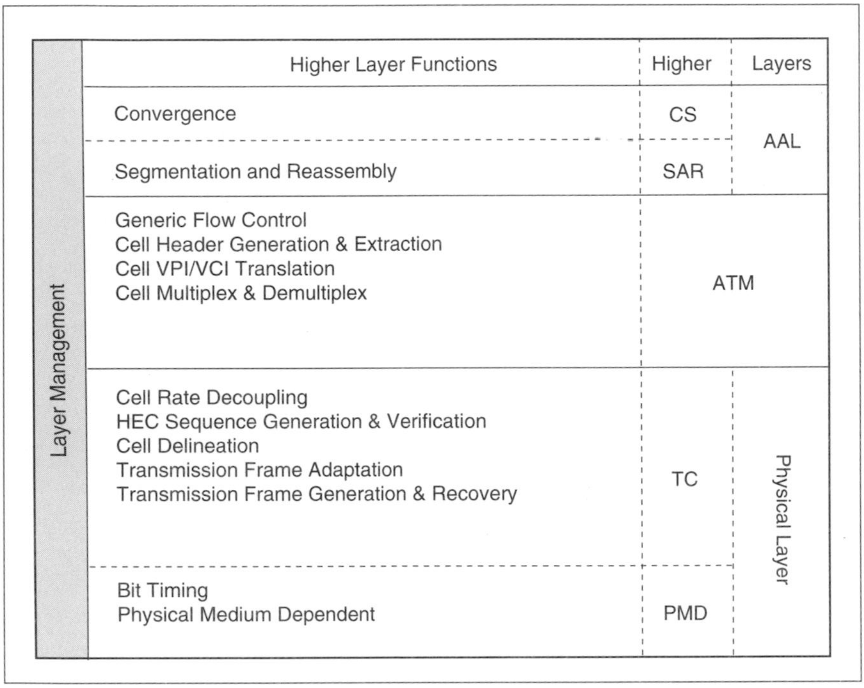

Higher Layer Functions	Higher	Layers
Convergence	CS	AAL
Segmentation and Reassembly	SAR	
Generic Flow Control Cell Header Generation & Extraction Cell VPI/VCI Translation Cell Multiplex & Demultiplex	ATM	
Cell Rate Decoupling HEC Sequence Generation & Verification Cell Delineation Transmission Frame Adaptation Transmission Frame Generation & Recovery	TC	Physical Layer
Bit Timing Physical Medium Dependent	PMD	

Layer Management

Figure 4.5: Functions of the different layers in the B-ISDN model.

video server to set top box. The major part of the functionality of the B-ISDN protocol is described in detail later, relative to the tasks of the user plane (i.e., the transport of information from point A to point B).

- The *control plane* is used when the signaling functions, such as call set up / disconnect, are done in order to enable a network where a connection of a specified quality can be setup on demand. (i.e., a Switched Virtual Circuit (SVC) network, as needed to enable services like video on Demand.)

- The *management plane* is divided in to two:

  - The *layer management* handles specific Operation and Maintenance (OAM) flows, for all layers. This could be network performance monitoring, or the detection and localization of faults. As an example, the Quality of Service (QoS) of the network can be monitored, including monitoring of the QoS of the ATM layer. As will be described in more detail later, it is possible to measure ATM layer QoS parameters, like cell loss and cell delay variation, via specific OAM cells in the ATM layer.

  - The *plane management* provides the coordination of the planes. To continue the example started above, the information flow from the layer management indicating a decline in ATM layer QoS is passed to the plane management, which receives similar types of information from the other layers such as the physical layer. In the case that serious problems occur, the plane management can then indicate this to a network management system.

The protocols are organized into several "layers." The layers have a clearly defined purpose, as well as a clearly defined interface to the other layers. Through the network, the layers communicate on a peer-to-peer basis. This means that the protocol layer "x" on the transmission side will communicate with layer "x" on the receiving side, via the information in the header or trailer fields contained in the PDU format for layer "x." (So the ATM layer implementation in the video server communicates with the ATM layer in a switch in the network.) It is important to understand that a protocol on layer "x" is not working with the payload of the layer "x" PDU. For example, the ATM layer is only concerned with information like VPI/VCI for multiplexing purposes. The actual payload can be passed directly to the AAL.

As seen in Fig. 4.5, the physical layer comprises two sublayers, the Transmission Convergence (TC) and the Physical Media Dependent (PMD) part. The AAL likewise comprises two main sublayers, (i.e., the Convergence Sublayer (CS) and the Segmentation and Reassembly (SAR) sublayers). Finally, the Higher Layers comprise all layers above the AAL, including services and end-to-end applications. This includes, for instance, the UNI and NNI signaling protocols, as well as the MPEG protocols. The higher layers also cover various methods for carrying LAN protocols, containing Internet traffic, for example to be transported via the B-ISDN.

4.5.2 Physical/Convergence Layer

For B-ISDN, a wide range of physical transmission methods are defined. The methods cover mainly three areas, (i.e., PDH, SONET/ SDH, and LAN oriented technologies). The role of the physical medium dependent layer and the transmission convergence layer will be dealt with separately in the next section, and so will some of the physical layer protocols most relevant to transmission of digital video in the B-ISDN. For PDH, the standards E1 and E3 for 2 Mbps and 34 Mbps respectively, are the most commonly used in Europe, DS-1 and DS-3 respectively for 1.5 Mbps and 45 Mbps are the most common in the US, and finally J2 for 6.3 Mbps is a commonly shown speed for transferring ATM cells on PDH in Japan. SONET and SDH are most commonly implemented at 155 Mbps (STS-3 or STM-1 for SONET and SDH respectively), but also 52 Mbps SONET STS-1 is used, and 622 Mbps STS-12 or STM-4 is gaining popularity on a general level, because of the demands for higher and higher bandwidth. The LAN oriented technologies comprise a range of different technologies, including 155 Mbps UTP-5 and the 25.6 Mbps 4B/5B block encoded ATM Forum standard.

This section will not be exhaustive in its description of all the possible physical specifications that can carry ATM cells. In contrast, it will be a relatively detailed description of probably the most important transmission specification for ATM cells—155 Mbps SDH/SONET followed by an overview of two of the most central PDH specifications, E3 and DS-3.

Transmission Convergence Layer

The Transmission Convergence (TC) part of the physical layer can, on a general level, be said to have the following functions:

- Adaption the cell flow to the bit rate of the PMD layer. This is done by inserting idle ATM cells as needed to fill the "unused bandwidth."

- Generation of the frame format, which is transmitted by the PMD layer.

- Processing of all overhead in the physical layer frame

- Insertion of ATM cells in, and extraction from, the physical layer frame.
- Recovery of the cell boundaries.
- Error check of the ATM cell header.

Physical Media Dependent Layer

The Physical Media Dependent (PMD) layer is the other sublayer of the physical layer. It defines the point to point transmission system used to link the network elements. It performs various functions, dependent of the requirements of the used physical medium, such as:

- Bit synchronization
- Line coding
- Electrical/optical conversion, if needed

4.5.3 SONET and SDH

The original development work that formed the SONET and SDH networks we deploy all over the world today was done in Bell Laboratories in the United States. The Bell Laboratories specified the concept of SONET (Synchronous Optical NETwork). In 1988, this was formed into a CCITT standard covering ANSI SONET and ETSI SDH (Synchronous Digital Network), with the help from European and Japanese standardization bodies. SONET was originally designed in such a way that it could easily cope with the existing North American DS-3 lines (45 Mbps). The lowest level in the SONET hierarchy is therefore STS-1, at a line speed at 52 Mbps in total, including SONET overhead. The differences between SONET and SDH are generally quite minimal. The main difference is that SDH uses a format called a VC-4 container to carry the payload, whereas SONET uses a VC-3 container, as this is better suited to carry the North American PDH rates. When ATM cells are transported however, SDH as well as SONET are using the VC-4 container. With respect to B-ISDN, the differences between SDH and SONET are essentially eliminated.

The reasons for deploying SDH/SONET in new networks are primarily that it is far more flexible in terms of multiplexing, (add-drop multiplexing, instead of time division multiplexing as in PDH), and that it has more "intelligence" in terms of network control and maintenance than PDH. SDH is specified in G.707, G.708 and G.709. SONET is specified in ANSI T1-105 and Bellcore GR-253.

SDH and SONET are defined for many speeds, even though 155 Mbps is the most commonly used for carrying ATM. In Table 4.1 the structure is shown.

A different way of using the payload than originally intended has been defined. It is called concatenation, and is marked at the rate by a "c" for "concatenated." STS-3, for instance, consists of 3 x STS-1 containers in the payload, each with overhead. This is practical if some level of multiplexing should take place at the SONET/SDH frame level. In B-ISDN, all multiplexing takes place on the ATM layer. Therefore, it was made possible to use the whole payload for cells, as in concatenated STS-3 (i.e., STS-3c).

Bit rate (Mbps)	CCITT (ITU-T) SDH STM – M = Synchronous Transport Module, level M	ANSI SONET STS – N = Synchronous Transport Signal, level N
51.84	-	STS-1
155.52	STM-1	STS-3
466.56	-	STS-9
622.08	STM-4	STS-12
933.12	-	STS-18
1244.16	-	STS-24
1866.24	-	STS-36
2488.32	STM-16	STS-48
4976.64	STM-32	STS-96
9953.28	STM-64	STS-192

Table 4.1: Different levels in SONET and SDH,
and the corresponding line speeds.

SONET STS-3c and SDH STM-1
Transmission Convergence
Sublayer

One of the most important physical layers for transporting ATM cells
is SDH STM-1 and SONET STS-3c. The Transmission Convergence
(TC) part of these protocols are essentially the function that connects
the ATM layer with the physical layer. The basic purpose of the

SONET/SDH TC is to generate the SONET or SDH frame, as well as to insert the ATM cells in the frame on the transmitting side and extract them from the frame on the receiving side. It furthermore performs the Header Error Control (HEC) to identify possible errors in the ATM cell header, and adapts the incoming ATM cell rate, with the capacity of SONET/SDH. 8000 SONET/SDH frames are sent per second, regardless of how many ATM cells need to be transported, so cell rate decoupling may be needed. This is performed by inserting empty ATM cells in the SDH container, "idle cells." Idle cells are characterized by having all 0s in the first four ATM header bytes, except for a 1 in the Cell Loss Priority (CLP field).

SDH STM-1 and SONET STS-3c
Frame Generation and Extraction

The way ATM cells are organized within the SONET or SDH frame can be illustrated by the following: At the transmitting side, the ATM cells are arranged within a container (C-4) that can carry 9 x 260 bytes, as illustrated in Fig. 4.6. The container is equipped with a 9 x 1 byte overhead, referred to as "path overhead," POH, and it now constitutes a virtual container (VC-4). The VC-4 is then mapped into a frame, called STM-1 or STS-3c, depending of whether SDH or SONET is used respectively. The frame has a 9 x 9 byte section overhead, called Section Overhead (SOH) in SDH, and Transport Overhead (TOH) in SONET, resulting in a total frame size of 2430 bytes. The frame is passed through the network, and once the frame reaches the receiving side, the reverse process essentially takes place, whereafter the extracted ATM cells are passed up to the ATM layer.

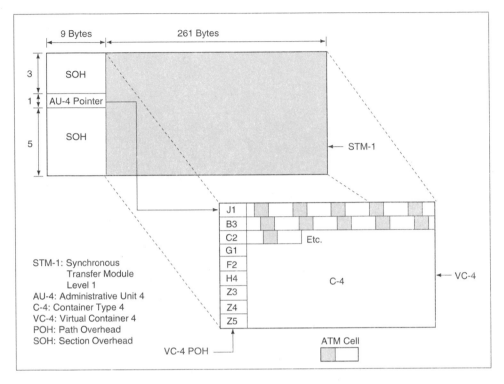

Figure 4.6: SONET/SDH framing when
transporting ATM cells: exemplified via SDH.

4.5.4 E3

E3 is the third level in the Plesiochronous Digital Hierarchy, commonly used in Europe. E3 lines carry four multiplexed E2 signals each of
8.448 Mbps, which again carry four E1 signals each of 2.048 Mbps. The
exact speed of E3 is 34.368 Mbps. Presently, in Europe, E3 is one of the

most important speeds for transmission of ATM cells, (along with SDH STM-1 in the core network).

There are currently three different ways to transmit ATM cells over E3—direct mapping, transmission in the PLCP frames, and, finally, using a relatively newly specified frame, described in ITU-T G.832. (The PLCP mapping is normally used in connection with the Switched Multimegabit Data Service (SMDS) in Metropolitan Area Networks (MANs).)

The new G.832 frame was specifically developed for transmission of ATM cells over the E3 interface, as the traditional frame was not especially well suited for this purpose. (It is based on a structure of an integral number of blocks with 4 bits—not 8 bits, as in one byte.) The G.832 frame has a size of 537 bytes, including 7 overhead bytes. The payload can therefore carry exactly 10 ATM cells, per frame. (10 x 53 = 530). This frame structure is transmitted 8000 times per second, regardless whether there is user traffic to be transported or not. Please refer to Fig. 4.7 for an illustration of the G.832 E3 frame.

4.5.5 DS-3

DS-3 is the third level in the PDH multiplexing hierarchy found in North America. DS-3 has a bandwidth of 44.736 Mbps and carries seven DS-2 channels of 6.312 Mbps, which again carries four DS-1 signals of 1.544 Mbps.

DS-3 is a highly deployed line type in Northern America, commonly used to carry ATM cells. The DS-3 speed is used for the SMDS as well, which like ATM also uses cells of 53 byte size. The convergence mechanism that was developed for SMDS, the Physical Layer Conver-

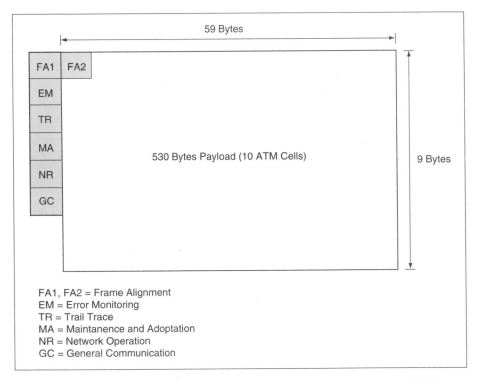

Figure 4.7: G.832 E3 frame structure used for carrying ATM.

gence Protocol, or PLCP, is therefore also used for ATM. The DS-3 PLCP format is specified in the Bellcore document TR-TSV-000773.

In the DS-3 frame format shown in Fig. 4.8, 12 ATM cells are contained, each preceded by 4 bytes of framing and control information. After the 12th cell, either 13 or 14 nibbles[1] are sent, to match the exact bit rate used. The frame structure is transmitted 8,000 times per second.

---

[1]Nibble = 4 bits.

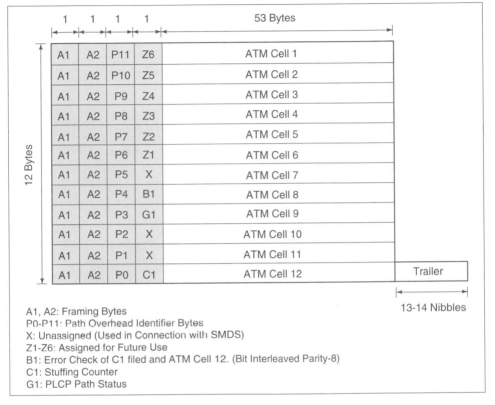

Figure 4.8: PLCP framing format used with DS-3.

4.5.6 Header Error Control (HEC)

Apart from adapting the ATM cell stream to fit into the physical speed and frame format, the TC sublayer performs error correction. ATM Transmission Convergence—Header Error Control (ATM TC-HEC), is the error correction method used in relation with the ATM cell header (HEC field). It is based on a form of the forward error correction type called SECDED or Single Error Correction Double Error Detection. The HEC process is capable of detecting single or multiple bit errors, as well as correcting single bit errors.[2]

The receiver's use of the HEC algorithm was made with the characteristics of optical transmission in mind. Optical transmission is, among other things, characterized by a mix of single bit errors, and relatively large error bursts. To be able to correct single bit errors, and minimize the risk of delivering cells with incorrect headers to the ATM layer under bursty error conditions, a structure with different "modes" is used. The default mode is a correction mode. If an error occurs it is either corrected or the cell is discarded. (In case of one single bit error, this is corrected—if there is one cell header with multiple errors, or several cell headers with errors, the cell (s) is/are discarded.) In both cases, the receiver enters "detection mode," where all cells with header errors are discharged. As soon as no errors are detected, the receiver returns to correction mode.

---

[2]The value placed in the HEC field is the result of the algorithm shown below.

$$\text{HEC} = Z\,((X^8)/(X^8 + X^2 + X + 1))\,XOR\,(01010101)$$

Note that it is the remainder of the fraction times the four first bytes of the ATM cell header (called "Z" here), XOR-ed with the 01010101 pattern, that is placed in the HEC field.

4.5.7 Cell Delineation

Along with error detection and correction, the ATM TC-HEC performs a cell delineation function. At the receiver side, it is necessary to be able to recognize the cell boundaries. This is done simply by using the correlation between the first four bytes of the header and the value in the HEC field. Scrambling of the ATM cell payload is furthermore used to reduce the probability that a part of the payload by chance imitates a cell header. When SDH or E3 PDH is used as the physical layer, the self synchronizing scrambling polynomial $X^{43} + 1$ is used.

Three different states for the cell delineation mechanism exist:

- Hunt state: Here the ATM cells are searched bit by bit until a correct combination of what is assumed to be the first four header bytes and the HEC value is found. The cell boundaries are now considered as identified, and the process goes to the "presync state."

- Presync state: Now the delineation check is continued cell by cell. If the assumed cell boundaries have been confirmed δ times consecutively, the location of the cell boundaries is considered as verified and the process enters the "sync" mode. The typical value for δ is 6.

- Sync state: In the Sync state α cell by cell check occurs. If an incorrect HEC is identified α times consecutively, the process returns to the hunt state. The typical value for α is 7.

4.5.8 ATM Layer

It is the ATM layer that makes it possible to transport services with highly different requirements over the same physical network in an efficient manner. The ATM layer performs the multiplexing and switching of ATM cells, carrying different services over different "virtual connections" through the network. Each different virtual connection is initially established according to the requirements of the specific service that is to be transmitted through it. The different virtual connections are identified via a local routing address assigned to all the ATM cells transmitted through a specific virtual connection. The local routing address is present in the ATM cell header as the Virtual Path Indicator (VPI) field and the Virtual Channel Indicator (VCI) field. A video service carried in the cells with the VPI/VCI value 10/20, for instance, can hereby easily be mixed with other video, voice or data services traveling over VPI/VCI value 11/21, and so forth. An ATM connection can, in principle, carry a number of virtual connections, equal to the number of VPI/VCI values available (at the UNI: 256 VPI values x 65,536 VCI values). Far less are used under normal circumstances, though.

ATM is a relatively simple protocol. As described earlier, an ATM PDU has a 48 byte payload and a 5 byte header. The header, shown in Fig. 4.9, reflects directly or indirectly on most of the aspects of ATM. There are two versions of the ATM cell—one used in the UNI and one used in the NNI. The difference is minimal—in the UNI the first four bits describes a GFC field, described more later. In the NNI, this field is added to the VPI field (i.e., there is no GFC field in the NNI).

Described on a general level, the ATM layer inserts local routing address information in the form of the VPI/VCI in the five byte ATM cell header, as well as information about the type of information the

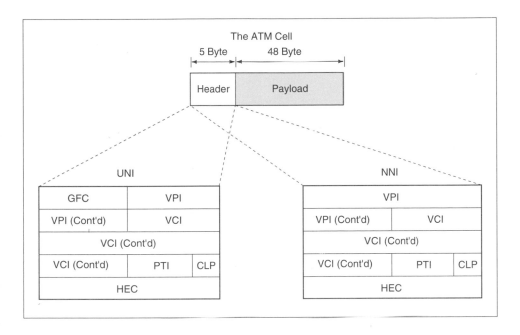

Figure 4.9: The ATM cell and the ATM cell
header at the UNI and the NNI.

cell carries. This can be user information or control information used
within the network. (So called OAM cells.) Cells of relatively lower
importance can be marked as "2 nd. class," by the means of a specific
bit in the header. As indicated earlier, the ATM layer performs cell
switching and multiplexing functions. The necessary control information is contained in the address field of the header. At the receiving
side, the reverse functions are performed by the ATM layer (i.e., cell
de-multiplexing and removal of the header, among other things).

VPI and VCI

ATM is a connection oriented protocol, in contrast to other so called connectionless protocols, as, for instance, Ethernet LANs. The difference is simply that in a connectionless protocol, the complete destination address is carried in each packet/cell, whereas, in connection oriented protocols, the connection between end users is set up via signaling before the exchange of user data starts. So, in this scenario, it is no longer necessary that each PDU carries the destination address; a local routing address is sufficient. As mentioned, the local routing address in ATM is called the VPI/VCI. The VPI/VCI should not be mistaken by the 20 byte ATM address described later on. The ATM address is a unique destination address, which is used mainly at the time the connection is set-up, whereas the VPI/VCI is typically changed as the cell is routed from switch to switch.

The information flow, coming from a number of sources, is multiplexed in the ATM layer, leaving one ATM cell flow. It is possible to identify the different connections, via the VPI/VCI field of the cell header. In ATM, there is a two-level address structure relating to Virtual Channels (VC) and Virtual Paths (VP). When an ATM cell is sent, it must follow certain VCs and VPs to reach its destination. The values of the relevant VP and VC are located in the VPI and the VCI field of the header respectively. VPs and VCs are not physical, but should be considered as a useful abstraction. A VC is normally the user end-to-end connection, whereas the VP can be considered as a B-ISDN traffic pipeline containing a number of VCs. See Fig. 4.10.

- Virtual channels: An end-to-end connection between two users will normally consist of a number of concatenated VC

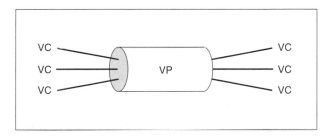

Figure 4.10: The relationship between VPs and VCs.

links, forming a VC *connection*. Each VC link has a given number, and every time the cell passes a VC switch, the value in the VCI field of the header is updated, according to the routing table in the switch. (The routing table describes the relationship between in and outgoing ATM cells, in terms of VPI/VCI, for all the ports on the switch. The routing table is updated regularly, as the signaling flow sets-up / tears-down connections.)

In practice, most connections are only needed for a limited period of time. When the connection is no longer needed, it will be taken down again, via the signaling procedures. Signaling in general, is a function of the control plane, shown in Fig. 4.4. Alternatively, the VC connection can be (semi-) permanent, leaving (semi-) permanent values in the routing translation table. This is set up by network administration, via various management plane functions, rather than by signaling. When a VC connection is established, several parameters are negotiated between the user and the network, such as bit rate, traffic profile, quality of service requirements, etc. If the requested

189

resources are available in the network, the connection is set-up. The traffic parameters can later be renegotiated.

In order to protect the network from congestion, the connections are monitored by the usage parameter control (UPC) function. If a user sends cells too quickly into the network, the UPC function may take action to discard the offending cells. UPC is also referred to as the "policing" function.

- *Virtual paths:* As stated, a VP is a "bundle" of VCs that follow the same route in the network. A VP link can be set up between two locations with high bandwidth demands, generally speaking, between a video server and the first switch. The VP concept is practical, as the connection is *logical* and independent of the actual physical connection. It gives flexibility, so that the logical structure can be rearranged according to traffic demands and the Quality of Service needed by different VCs. Using VPs furthermore reduce the need for VC switching capability, where there is no need for it (i.e., in the paths of traffic that follow the same route).

GFC

Generic Flow Control (GFC), is a header field used only at the UNI (the customer premises). It may be used for media access control for terminals in an ATM LAN, for instance. As soon as the ATM cell passes the NNI (the public network), the GFC field is interpreted differently (i.e., as a part of the VPI field). As a consequence, the GFC information is not transferred through the public network and can therefore only be used between the UNI elements.

PTI

The payload type indicator (PTI) is available to identify the type of data in the payload field of the cell. This can be either data for use internally in the network or normal user data. The eight possible combinations are shown in Table 4.2.

As can be seen, the first four combinations are used in conjunction with AAL 5 in order to indicate which ATM cell in a cell stream carries the last part of a higher layer PDU.* The next two, "100" and "101," indicates if the cell is a F5 OAM cell. (F4 OAM cells are not indicated via the PTI field). The last two combinations are reserved for future

PTI value	Meaning
"000"	User data, no congestion, SDU Type = 0 (Payload is AAL 5 Body Cell)
"001"	User data, no congestion, SDU Type = 1 (Payload is AAL 5 Body Cell)
"010"	User data, congestion, SDU Type = 0 (Payload is AAL 5 Body Cell)
"011"	User data, congestion, SDU Type = 1 (Payload is AAL 5 Body Cell)
"100"	Segment OAM F5 Flow Cell
"101"	End-to-End F5 Flow Cell
"110"	Reserved for traffic control and resource management
"111"	Reserved for future functions

Table 4.2: PTI field contents and meaning.

use. In the ATM layer there are two types of operations and maintenance (OAM) cells, relating to VCs or VPs, that performs the following:

- OAM cells, type F4: VP performance monitoring, such as cell loss ratio, and monitoring of path availability.
- OAM cells, type F5: VC performance and availability monitoring.
- OAM cells can be used within a network segment, between B-TE and LEX for instance, or over end-to end connections. The F5 cells are identified by the PTI, as described above. The F4 cells use a reserved VC value (i.e., VC = 3 for F4 cells in a network segment and VC = 4 for end-to-end F4 cells).

CLP

Cell Loss Priority (CLP) is used to indicate if the cell has relatively
lower priority. In the case of video or voice transmission, the loss of
some cells may not be of significant importance to the quality of the
transmission. The low importance cells are marked with a "1" in the
CLP, and are discarded first in the case of network congestion. The per-
centage of low priority cells can be negotiated at call setup via the signaling messages.

HEC

Header Error Control (HEC) checks the ATM cell header for errors.
The value is calculated and inserted via the transmission convergence
sublayer. The HEC field also allows the network elements to achieve
cell level synchronization, as described earlier.

4.5.9 ATM Layer Quality of Service (QoS)

Digital video services, along with all other services in B-ISDN, are dependent on the performance and the quality of service the ATM layer can provide. The information transported through the ATM layer of the B-ISDN network can be subject to various sorts of "impairments." These impairments can be caused by the various network elements and are essentially due to the fact that ATM is based on statistical multiplexing. This can give the effect that the users of the B-ISDN network will experience a degradation in the quality of the service they are using. An example of this could be that the viewers experience degraded picture quality in the form of distorted colors or blockiness, possibly along with a distorted audio signal.

ATM uses statistical multiplexing in order to utilize network resources in an efficient manner. Typically, a combination of many variable bitrate and constant bitrate connections are multiplexed together via the ATM layer. Statistical multiplexing does have the drawback, however, that situations can occur where ATM cells must be dropped, due to network congestion. Furthermore, delay can be caused, for instance, by big buffers and long transmission lines. Cell delay variation can be caused by varying buffer size/usage of the network, along with varying congestion conditions.

To make a dialog possible between network users and network/service providers, a set of metrics has been defined, Quality of Service parameters, normally referred to as QoS parameters. The user on one side wishes to get his service, like Video on Demand (VoD) in the quality payed for, or at least an acceptable quality. He/she does not want to experience things like frozen pictures and distorted sound. At the same time he/she probably could not care less about how the network provider chooses to provide the service. The network/service provider has major investments in network equipment and copper/fibre cables. He/she wishes to utilize this in an optimal way, so the bandwidth is used as much as possible by paying customers all the time. This gives two different points of view on the same thing—the quality of service. The parameters are:

- Cell Error Ratio
- Severely Errored Cell Block Ratio
- Cell Loss Ratio
- Cell Misinsertion Rate
- Cell Delay
- Cell Delay Variation (cell jitter)

The effects of these parameters on transmitted MPEG-2 compressed video and audio are quite different. With respect to cell errors, the error correction algorithms in digital video networks, for instance, implementations of the Reed-Solomon Forward Error Correction (FEC), raise the error resilience of the system from a bit error rate of 10^{-4} to 10^{-11}, typically. (As a rule of thumb, an unprotected MPEG-2 transport stream should not be exposed to conditions causing a bit error rate of more than 10^{-11}. Higher bit error rates start to cause serious problems in decoding the signal properly.)

To cope with bursts of cell errors, a method for spreading the bursts of errors over a large block of data has been made, so that the FEC mechanism can correct the errors. It is referred to as "interleaving." It is used together with the FEC, as described in ITU-T J.82 and I.363. Cell errors, or bursts of cell errors ("blocks" of cell errors), may therefore not always be a serious problem, if the interleaving and FEC is used. The system may hereby be able to recover the information loss without any significant disturbance of the picture quality.

In the case where no FEC is used, or where the limit of how many errors the FEC can correct is exceeded, the effects can however be drastic. This is also referred to as the *cliff effect*. (The cliff effect is describing the way digital video fails. An example: One moment the user may experience a perfect picture and sound, even though there can be many (corrected) errors in the bit stream. If the error rate increases just slightly, the FEC may have reached the point where no more errors can be corrected successfully, and as a result, the user may suddenly experience badly impaired video and audio.)

Cell loss can be a more serious problem as more information is lost, especially if no FEC implementations are used. Even though loss of one ATM cell only mean loss of 48 bytes of information, this can still have quite some effect. First of all, the 48 bytes are normally just a small part of an upper layer PDU. It could, for example, be a MPEG-2 transport stream packet, containing part of a PES packet, which again contains a slice. Hereby the complete slice is erred due to the loss of one ATM cell. If the slice happened to have been part of an I-frame, the erred slice may stay on the screen for up to 1/3 of a second, if it is reused by the following P- and B-frames (more than enough time to make it noticeable for the viewer). In the case that the lost cell contained the start code for a GOP, the effect could be even more severe, due to loss of synchronization.

The use of the FEC and interleaving method described above allows recovery of up to 4 lost ATM cells out of 128 cells. Generally considered, it is probably equally important to focus on how often cell loss or cell errors occur, compared to the exact number of cell errors/lost cells. Cell misinsertion, is normally not a problem encountered in ATM networks with commercially available switches.

Long constant cell delay may be a problem if the application is interactive, as relatively long waiting time may be experienced. High cell delay variation (CDV) is under all circumstances a problem in MPEG-2-based video applications, as it may violate the timing model used by the MPEG-2 systems layer. CDV can cause PCR jitter, which again can cause degraded picture quality, seen as color distortion or blockiness. Also, the CDV can be addressed by using the AAL-1 encapsulation. Please refer to the section dealing with "Video in Broadband Networks," for more details on the AAL-1 and AAL-5 encapsulation methods, which are used when transporting MPEG-2 over the B-ISDN network.

The QoS of a specific virtual connection in the B-ISDN network is specified and negotiated between the end user and the network, when the connection is initiated. For the UNI side, this is done via the signaling procedures, described in ITU-T Q.2931 or the ATM Forum documents. As soon as the request passes from the user part of the network into the public part of the network, an NNI signaling protocol takes over. This could typically be the B-ISUP protocol defined by ITU-T or the B-ICI protocol defined by the ATM Forum.

The process essentially follows the following pattern: The end user requests set up to a connection through the network with a specific QoS. As this setup message passes through the network over the UNI and the NNI, typically via several switches, all the involved network elements verify that the requested QoS can be honored. If one of the network elements is unable to provide the requested QoS, the connection is rejected. (If, for instance, a switch is already heavily loaded with traffic, it may not have the necessary resources to also handle the requested connection.) If the connection is rejected, the user can try again immediately requesting a lower QoS or wait until a later time. For more details on signaling procedures, please refer to the later section dealing with B-ISDN signaling.

4.5.10 ATM Adaptation Layer (AAL)

The ATM layer has to cope with services with vastly different requirements. As an example, an MPEG compressed video stream is highly sensitive to cell delay variation, as it typically causes PCR jitter. In contrast, transmission of data (like a file transfer, or transfer of Internet information) is hardly influenced by even high levels of cell delay variation. Therefore, there has to be a function that makes it possible for the ATM layer to respect the different requirements of the different services. This is the job of the AAL.

The information coming from the different services, the service layer PDUs, are equipped with a header that holds the relevant information about of the following functions (depending of the requirements of the service):

- Error check: As the ATM layer has no payload error check functions, this function is needed here.

- Sequence integrity check: Even though cell sequence integrity is preserved within a virtual channel, some of the AAL protocols check that no cells are put in incorrect order.

- Multiplexing information: In the cases where several B-TEs share a single virtual connection, multiplexing information is needed.

- Timing compensation: In the case of real-time applications, it is necessary to cope with the effects of the missing timing relationship between the end-to end application and the network clock.

The AAL PDUs are now segmented into 48 byte blocks that will fit into the payload part of the ATM cells. A number of AAL protocols have been developed to meet the requirements of different services. AALs have been developed for services that require a constant delay (e.g., telephony, done via AAL-1). Other AALs have been developed mainly for data communication applications (i.e., where error detection, rather than timing compensation, is relevant). The AAL-3/4 and AAL-5 are used here. The AAL-2 is foreseen to be used for transmission of variable bitrate video in the B-ISDN. Basically, four types of AAL protocols exist, as shown in Fig. 4.11.

- Class A: circuit emulation, constant bit rate video
- Class B: variable bit-rate video and audio
- Class C: connection-oriented data transfer
- Class D: connectionless data transfer

The two AALs presently used for transfer of digital video are AAL-1 and AAL-5. (The AAL-2, as mentioned, was originally intended to be used for video but has not yet been sufficiently developed.) The

Service Parameters	Class A	Class B	Class C	Class D
Timing Compensation	Required		Not Required	
Bit Rate	Constant	Variable		
Connection Mode	Connection Oriented			Connection-less
Example of Application	Video or Voice Circuit Emulation	VBR Video	Connection Oriented Data Transfer. E.g. Frame Relay	Connection-less Data Transfer. E.g. SMDS
AAL Type	AAL-1	AAL-2	AAL-3/4 AAL-5	AAL-3/4

Figure 4.11: Relationships between services and AALs.

following is an introduction to the function of AAL-1 and AAL-5. For the specific details on how the MPEG-2 TS packets are handled, please refer to the section dealing with "Video in Broadband Networks" on page 101.

AAL-1

AAL-1 has a range of capabilities included, that allow it to "emulate" a constant bit rate connection. This is useful as many technologies, including video codecs, have been designed to or adapted to the characteristics of the existing PDH network. The MPEG-2 transport stream, for instance, works under the assumption that there is a fixed constant delay between transmitter and receiver.

The PDH network is based on time division multiplexing and offers a fixed bandwidth with fixed constant delay. As ATM is asynchronous, AAL-1 is equipped with additional information, such as time stamps and sequence numbers, to perform the adaptation. Hereby, the effects of cell delay variation, cell misinsertion, cell loss, and other ATM layer caused impairments can be dealt with.

AAL-1 can handle transfer of data in two modes: Unstructured Data Transfer (UDT) or Structured Data Transfer (SDT). When UDT is used, the AAL expects the data flow to be a bit stream with associated clock synchronization. Using SDT, the data flow is expected to be structured in octet "blocks," such as a time division multiplexed signal with "n" channels of 64 Kbps. Normal telephone networks carry n channels with voice sampled 8,000 per second. In SDT it is therefore necessary to include a "pointer" in the SAR payload, indicating the beginning of the next octet block. The PDU structure differs slightly depending whether SDT or UDT mode is used. The described pointer is placed in the first byte of every other AAL-1 payload, as illustrated in Fig. 4.12.

CS and SAR

Like all other AALs, AAL-1 is split into two sublayers, the segmentation and reassembly sublayer (SAR), and the convergence sublayer (CS). The function of the CS covers the generation and recovery of timing information (i.e., it can compensate for the effects of cell delay variation, it takes care of cell misinsertion, cell loss and cell mis-sequencing, and it flags possible error conditions to the management plane).

On the transmitting side, the SAR segments the CS PDUs into blocks of 47 bytes of payload and adds the one byte header to fit the 48

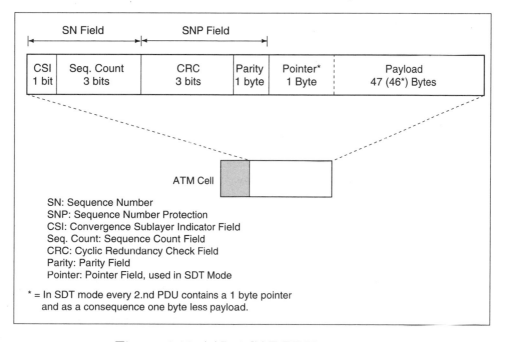

Figure 4.12: AAL-1 SAR PDU structure.

byte format, which the payload field of the ATM cell has. On the receiving side, the reverse process takes place—the header is stripped off, and the blocks of 47 bytes are re-built into the original CS PDU. The SAR has the function of generating and verifying the error protection fields, including possible 1 bit error correction.

The functions of the overhead bytes of the AAL-1 SAR PDU are:

- CSI: Indicates whether SDT or UDT mode is used by setting the value to "1" in every 2nd PDU (the even numbered

PDUs carry the one byte pointer shown in Fig. 4.12). The CSI field also carries timing information in the odd numbered PDUs. This is done via a 4 bit SRTS (Synchronous Residual Time Stamp) carried over four PDUs. So in total, one 4 bit time stamp is received over 8 PDUs. This information, together with the common ATM network clock, makes it possible to reconstruct the original clock sequence at the receiver side.

- Sequence Count: In order to identify mis-sequenced, misinserted and missing ATM cells, a modulo-8 counter is placed in the sequence count field.

- CRC: As the sequence count and timing recovery information fields carry vital information for the AAL-1 function, this is protected by a CRC-3 field. It is a so called SECDED function, (Single Error Correction, Double Error Detection)—it can correct single bit errors and identify multibit errors.

- Parity: To increase the protection against errors even further, a parity bit covering the first seven bits of the header (i.e., the CSI, the Sequence Count and the CRC-3 field) is applied.

AAL-5

AAL-5 was originally intended for connection oriented data transfer, but has evolved to address MPEG-2 compressed video also. AAL-5 is an extremely efficient protocol with very little overhead. On the other hand, it has no function that can cope with timing relationships,

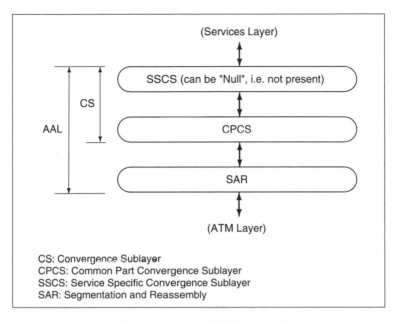

Figure 4.13: Structure of AAL-5 sublayers.

mis-sequenced ATM cells, nor can it carry more than one connection per VC, such as for instance AAL-3/4.

As shown in Fig. 4.13, AAL-5 is divided in two major parts:

- Convergence Sublayer (CS)
  - Service Specific Convergence Sublayer (SSCS) that can be *Null*
  - Common Part Convergence Sublayer (CPCS)
- Segmentation And Reassembly (SAR)

The services layer PDU enters the AAL, SSCS, or/and CPCS control information is added, leaving a CS PDU that is segmented by the SAR into blocks of 48 bytes. These blocks fit into the payload field of the ATM cell. At the receiving side, the user data is reassembled to its original form, and the CPCS control information is removed and dealt with.

CS and SAR

The CPCS format, and its relation to SAR and the ATM cell format, can be seen in Fig. 4.14.

The CPCS payload containing the services layer PDU/AAL SDU is of variable size up to 65,536 bytes. The functions of the CPCS trailer are:

- Pad: Padding is done in order to make the total length of the AAL SDU a multiple of 48.

- CPCS-UU: Direct information transfer from user to user on the CPCS layer is enabled by the CPCS-UU field.

- CPI: Mostly for further study. A function of the field that has been defined is to align the trailer to 64 bits.

- Length: It is necessary for the AAL on the receiving side to know the length of the valid data in the payload to be able to discard the padding. The size of CPCS payload is therefore put into the length field.

- CRC-32: Error check to verify that no errors have occurred during transmission, a CRC value of the CPCS PDU is calculated.

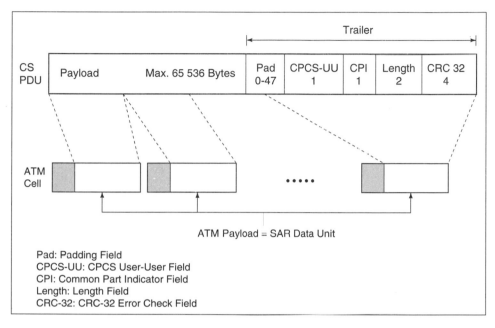

Figure 4.14: AAL-5 CPCS format ("CS PDU") and the ATM cell.

The SAR function takes care of dividing the CPCS PDU into blocks of 48 bytes, as mentioned. No SAR overhead is added in AAL-5. The only control information relating to this function is placed in the "PTI" field of the ATM cell header. Essentially, two conditions can be indicated in the PTI field, namely whether the ATM cell payload carries the beginning or the continuation of a CPCS PDU, or the end of it. This is also referred to as "body cell" or "end cell." In this way, the loss of an ATM cell will only cause loss of the CPCS PDU it is a part of.

4.5.11 B-ISDN Services

The services layer accepts data from an end-to-end user "application," such as a video user on the one side and a video server at the other side. It passes the information down to the AAL for further handling on the transmitting side. At the receiving side, the AAL passes the incoming information back up to the services layer, whereafter it can be delivered to the other user, server, etc. The MPEG-2 systems layer can be considered to reside in the services layer, but, in general, the services can take the form of connection oriented or connectionless data transfer, video or voice, as described earlier. Apart from handling user data, the services layer is the access point for network management, allowing network administrators to configure and monitor the network. The services layer is also the layer where signaling resides.

Signaling

To make a B-ISDN accommodate appealing services, the possibility for the user to set up a connection on demand is in almost all cases necessary. The ability to set up connections on demand in order to create Switched Virtual Circuits (SVCs) relies on signaling protocols. In some of the very early field trial B-ISDN networks, Permanent Virtual Circuits (PVCs) were used, as signaling capabilities were not supported by the network equipment. PVCs are connections that are set up manually via the network management system, typically for longer duration. The usage of PVCs was practical in the beginning, especially as the number of connections was relatively small. In commercial networks, however, it is necessary for the network to be capable of setting-up and maintaining hundreds or thousands of connections simultaneously. The only way to enable that and at the same time make efficient use of the network resources is to use signaling.

After an overview of the different signaling protocols, this section will use UNI signaling, more specifically the ITU-T variant, (as opposed to the similar ATM Forum variants) to exemplify the function and protocol structure of signaling in B-ISDN.

Signaling procedures are used all the way through the network— from one user's terminal equipment to the other user's terminal equipment, or from user to video server, etc., via one or more switches. Two major groups of signaling protocols can be distinguished:

- UNI signaling (i.e., the signaling protocols working between the user and the first access switch (LEX) in the network).

- NNI signaling, (i.e., the signaling protocols working between the switches (LEXs and TEXs) in the network).

Both ITU-T and the ATM Forum are active in the standardization work for both UNI signaling and NNI signaling. ITU-T has specified Q.2931 as layer 3 UNI signaling protocol, and Q.2130 (SSCF) and Q.2110 (SSCOP) as layer 2 protocols. For NNI ITU-T has defined the B-ISUP (Broadband ISDN User Part) as the signaling protocol. The B-ISUP resides on top of a protocol called MTP-3 (Message Transfer Part—3), which again uses the SSCOP via a special version of the SSCF.

The ATM Forum has specified two layer 3 UNI signaling protocols, known as UNI 3.0 and UNI 3.1. The UNI 3.1 uses the ITU-T Q.2130 and Q.2110 as layer 2 protocols, as can be seen in Fig. 4.15, whereas the UNI 3.0 uses two special protocols, Q.SAAL-1 and Q.SAAL-2. For NNI protocols, the ATM Forum is active in defining an alternative to ITU-T's B-ISUP protocol, called B-ICI, or Broadband Inter Carrier Interface. For large private networks, the ATM Forum has identified the need for a NNI signaling protocol to be used between private switches, called P-NNI, or Private NNI.

UNI Signaling

The UNI signaling protocols can be described via a layered model, as seen in Fig. 4.15, covering the signaling layer, the Service Specific Conversion Function (SSCF), and the the Service Specific Connection Oriented Protocol (SSCOP). The SSCOP layer PDUs are carried via AAL-5 and on the ATM the UNI signaling messages are typically transported via VPI/VCI value 0/5. The function of the different layers are:

- Signaling Layer: To provide the ability to establish clear virtual ATM connections at the UNI on a dynamically basis.

- SSCF: To provide mapping between the signaling protocols and the SSCOP. The SSCF does not transfer or receive information to or from the SSCF on the adjacent side.

- SSCOP: To provide an assured connection from end to end. The SSCOP will guarantee the delivery (via possible retransmission), as well as the sequence of the transmitted information. This is necessary as the AAL does not make this guaranteed transfer, which the signaling layer relies upon.

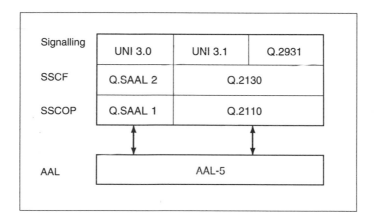

Figure 4.15: UNI signaling stack.

The signaling procedure sets up a connection according to the specified traffic contract between the initiating user, the network and the "receiving" side. The traffic contract describes the connection in great detail. Aspects such as peak cell rate, sustainable cell rate, maximum burst size, etc. are normally covered, along with other parameters describing the QoS of the connection, what AAL type is used, and finally the 20 byte ATM addresses of the called and calling party.

UNI Signaling Message Flow

Information exchange on the signaling level takes place via messages. Fig. 4-16 shows an example of the signaling flow in the case where a connection is established. The initiating side starts the process by transmitting a "setup" message. The setup message, which contains a description of the desired connection as outlined above, passes through the network, possibly via a number of switches and the NNI, to the

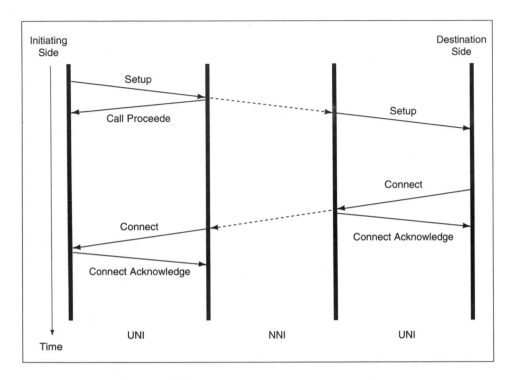

Figure 4.16: UNI signaling flow, exemplified
by a connection establishment.

destination identified by a 20 byte long ATM address. When the UNI
messages passes the NNI, they get translated into the relevant NNI
signaling messages, and vice versa when the UNI on the other side is
reached.

In the case that the connection can be honored through the whole
network, and the destination accepts the request, the destination side
issues a "connect" message. The connect message contains, among other

things, a number that uniquely identifies this specific connection, the "call reference value." This is needed as more connections can be established simultaneously to the same server for instance. The connect message is transported back to the initiator and the connection is formed through the network.

Now all involved components, switches, terminal equipment, and so on, have information on what specific VPI/VCI this specific connection uses. The VPI/VCI values for one connection can typically change several times through the network.

The above describes the main logical flow when establishing a connection. There is, as shown in Fig. 4.16 a flow of other messages, specifically the "call proceed" and "connect acknowledge." Call proceed is a message issued by the first switch the setup message reaches. The function of the message is essentially to inform the originator what VPI/VCI the call has been assigned to between the local switch and the originator. The connect acknowledge messages in the figure are issued as an indication that the connection is accepted by the local switch on the destination side, as well as by the originator, once the connect message is received.

UNI Signaling Messages and IEs

The UNI signaling PDU structure is shown in Fig. 4.17. The general format covers 9 bytes plus a number of Information Elements (IEs). Each message type can have a number of mandatory and optional IEs appended. The IEs contain the information describing the desired bandwidth of the connection, the QoS, and the ATM address of the calling and called party.

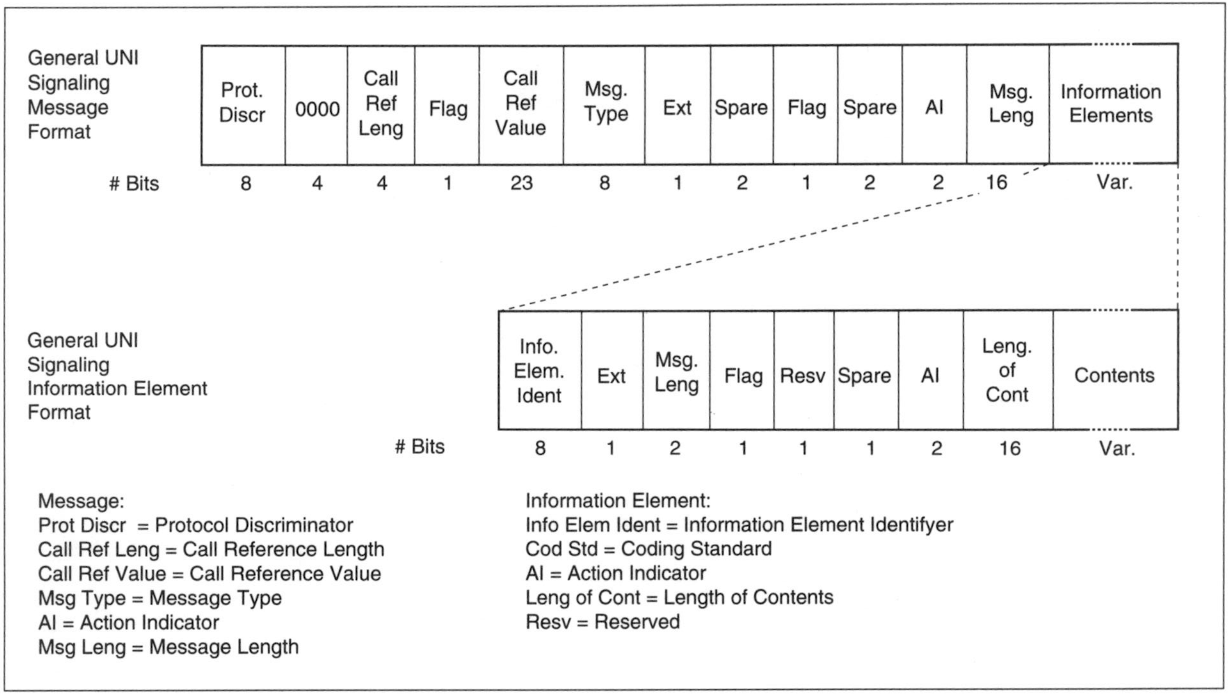

General UNI Signaling Message Format

Prot. Discr	0000	Call Ref Leng	Flag	Call Ref Value	Msg. Type	Ext	Spare	Flag	Spare	AI	Msg. Leng	Information Elements
8	4	4	1	23	8	1	2	1	2	2	16	Var.

Bits

General UNI Signaling Information Element Format

Info. Elem. Ident	Ext	Msg. Leng	Flag	Resv	Spare	AI	Leng. of Cont	Contents
8	1	2	1	1	1	2	16	Var.

Bits

Message:
Prot Discr = Protocol Discriminator
Call Ref Leng = Call Reference Length
Call Ref Value = Call Reference Value
Msg Type = Message Type
AI = Action Indicator
Msg Leng = Message Length

Information Element:
Info Elem Ident = Information Element Identifyer
Cod Std = Coding Standard
AI = Action Indicator
Leng of Cont = Length of Contents
Resv = Reserved

Figure 4.17: General structure of the UNI signaling message and information element.

Please refer to Table 4.3 for a description of the different fields found in the UNI signaling message format, and Table 4.4 for a description of the different fields found in the information element format.

PDU Field	Description
Protocol Discriminator	Unique value that describes what protocol the message should be interpreted as. To identify Q.2931 messages, the value "9" is used.
Call Reference Length	This field is by default set to "3," identifying the length of the following call reference value field in bytes.
Flag	The flag, which is actually the first byte of the call reference value field, identifies which side of the connection that assigned the call reference value.
Call Reference Value	Unique number that identifies a given connection. This is needed, as several calls may be handled simultaneously.
Message Type	Identifies what the function of the message is, for instance, a "setup" message.
Ext, Spare, Flag, Spare, AI	This collection of fields indicates how the message should be handled by the receiver in case the message can not be identified.

Table 4.3: Meaning of the different fields
found in the UNI signaling message,

PDU Field	Description
Information Element Identifier	Identifies how the PDU should be interpreted (as which information element). For instance, Quality of Service parameter, called party number, etc.
Coding Standard	Identifies which standard the IE follows (e.g., ITU-T).
Spare and Action Indicator	The two fields together indicate a specific possible action, for instance, to discard the IE or the whole message.
Length of Contents	Identifies the number of bytes that follow this field, in the contents field.

Table 4.4: Meaning of the different fields found
in the UNI signaling Information Element.

The ITU-T have, with Q.2931, defined a whole range of messages that can be used at the UNI. The complete range can be seen In Fig. 4.18. According to the needs of the specific implementation, it is possible to use only a subset of the available message types. The IEs that are used with the Q.2931 messages as shown in the same figure.

Message types in Q.2931	Information Element Types used in Q.2931
Call Proceeding	
Connect	AAL Parameters
Connect Acknowledge	ATM User cell rate
Setup	Broadband bearer capability
Release	Broadband high layer information
Release Complete	Broadband low layer information
Restart	Broadband repeat indicator
Restart Acknowledge	Broadband sending complete
Status	Call state
Status Engineering	Called party number
Alerting	Called party subaddress
Notify	Calling party number
Progress	Calling party subaddress
Setup Acknowledge	Cause
Infomation	Commection identifier
	Transit network selection
	Restart indicator
	Quality of service parameter
	End to end transit delay
	Notification indicator
	OAM traffic descriptor

Figure 4.18: Message types and the information element types used in Q.2931 UNI signaling.

To Get More Details . . .

To get more detailed information on the B-ISDN network technologies, the typical starting point would be the ITU standards, as for example [9-22, 41, 48, 50, 51, 52], along with the ATM Forum standards, as for example [6, 7]. Other books dealing with the subject are R. Händel, M. Huber and S. Schröder's *ATM Networks* [5] which can be recommended, along with Martin de Prycker's *Asynchronous Transfer Mode—Solution for Broadband ISDN* [3]. Apart from that, information can be found via the WWW. For instance, several FAQs are dealing with ATM and B-ISDN.

5

Access Networks

5.1 Access Networks— On a Page

The distribution mechanism covering the last few hundred meters to the end users is one of the major issues when implementing a digital video network. The new digital video services have requirements to the network that are relatively demanding in terms of bandwidth and, in the case of VoD, also in terms of interactivity. This must be accommodated in a cost efficient manner to make the new services attractive to the end user. At the same time, other services, like telephone or data communication, must be provided, typically over the same infrastructure. The access network, connecting the end user with the core network, performs the distribution of the above mentioned services.

This chapter first sets out to define the basic functions of access networkas in general, whereafter, a general introduction to the most discussed access network structures, in terms of network architecture and capabilities, follows. The access network types described are:

- Hybrid Fiber Coax
- Asymmetrical Digital Subscriber Line/Very High Speed Digital Subscriber Line
- Fiber To The Curb
- Fiber To The Home
- Satellite and Terrestrial Distribution
- Multipoint Multichannel Distribution System/Local Multipoint Distribution System

5.2 Access Networks— The Basics

The access network essentially performs the function of transporting data from the core network to the end user and, in the case of interactive services, also in the reverse direction. It is the so called "last mile" to the end user. The access network will typically carry not only the services based on MPEG-2 compressed digital video, but Internet access, telephony, and analogue television services.

A multitude of different access network architectures have already been outlined and specified by DAVIC, among others. The reason for not having one universal access network specification is that many different cabling architectures are already installed. The investment these installations represent makes it a necessary to accommodate them in the specifications. It is, to say the least, a time and money consuming exercise to lay a whole new cabling network out to all users in an area, an exercise normally avoided where possible. The different access network structures such as Hybrid Fiber Coax (HFC), Fiber To The Curb (FTTC), Fiber To The Home (FTTH), Asymmetrical Digital Subscriber Line (ADSL), and Multichannel Multipoint Distribution System (MMDS), all have different characteristics that make each type especially well suited to use under specific circumstances—and less well suited to use under other circumstances.

The many access network architectures that have been proposed generally cover the same main elements. The overall generic structure has been described by DAVIC, as seen in Fig. 5.1.

219

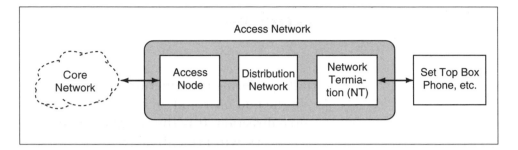

Figure 5.1: Generic access network model.

The access network normally consists of the local access node connected to the core network (via a LEX placed at the periphery of the core network), the distribution network, and the network termination (NT) located at the end user.

- The access node acts as the connection point to the—typically ATM-based—core network. It performs functions such as conversion of line speed and transmission protocol format to/from the distribution network.

- The distribution network takes care of the transport and distribution of the signals to/from the end user. The network can be wireless or based on optical fibers, twisted pair copper cables or coaxial cables, or even combinations. The cable-based networks can either have a star-based or a shared media topology.

- The Network Termination (NT) is considered as the demarcation point between the public and the private domain. The network termination can be a *passive NT* (i.e., a passive "plug in the wall" with no built-in functionality, apart from being the connecting point for the users equipment). In the case where more functionality is needed, as for instance conversion between media types, the device is called *an active NT*.

5.3 Access Network Types

5.3.1 Introduction

In the following section, a general overview of some of the most discussed access network technologies is given:

- FTTC (Fiber To The Curb)
- ADSL (Asymmetrical Digital Subscriber Line)/ VDSL (Very High Speed Digital Subscriber Line)
- HFC (Hybrid Fiber Coax)
- FTTH (Fiber To The Home)
- Satellite and Terrestrial distribution
- MMDS (Multipoint Multichannel Distribution System)/ LMDS (Local MDS)

Access network technologies can be grouped on an overall level, as shown in Fig. 5.2. A distinction is made on whether the access network is wireless or cable-based. Within the cable-based technologies a further distinction is made according to the topology used. HFC is based on access to a shared media, whereas technologies such as FTTC, ADSL, and VDSL are using dedicated access (i.e., a star architecture where each user has a dedicated wire between his or her premises, and the central office or ONU). Within this group of technologies, a further

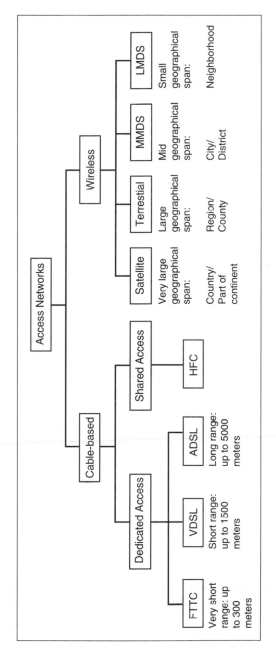

Figure 5.2: Example of commonly discussed access network types.

distinction can be made on the possible geographical span of each technology. As an example, FTTC typically reaches up to about 300 meters, whereas ADSL can cover up to 5-6 kilometers between the central office and the end user.

A similar distinction can be made with wireless technologies. As an example, satellite broadcasts can cover an area with a diameter of thousands of kilometers, whereas LMDS only covers a few kilometers. It should be noted that satellite and terrestrial distribution are well established technologies for transmission in a distributive manner, presently used essentially for broadcast services. In this sense, they differ from the other access technologies mentioned in this section, as these technologies (FTTC, LMDS, etc.) are relatively new technologies that can accommodate a two way information flow, not solemnly distribution (i.e., broadcast). For satellite and terrestrial networks to accommodate interactive services, some sort of upstream or return path has to be defined. This could be via the POTS or via the N-ISDN lines, as seen with MMDS.

It is important to realize that there still seems to be some ambiguity in the meaning of the different new types of access networks. There is no "one" type of the access network types, like a global standard for HFC for instance. There have been taken, and there still are taken, various approaches for HFC, as well as the other new access network types. The overall structure is similar, but many of the details are done differently. Typically, aspects such as framing, whether ATM cells are carried over the access network or not, usage of the frequency spectrum, and bandwidth, may differ from implementation to implementation.

As several variants of the mentioned access network types exist, this section therefore deals with the access network technologies on mainly the general level. For more detailed information on the different specific implementations, see for instance the DAVIC specifications. For broadcast type services, for instance the DVB-C, DVB-S, or DVB-T specifications can be studied. (Please see the List of References on page 279.)

5.3.2 FTTC

The FTTC utilizes a structure based on optical fibers from the central office, connected to the ATM-based core network, to the curb where the Optical Network Units (ONUs) are located. The fibers typically carry digital services, such as VoD. The downstream information flow is passed from the ATM-based core network via an edge switch (LEX) before it enters the access network via the access node in the central office. The upstream follows the same path but in the reverse direction. The ONUs are also connected to the central office via a coaxial cable. This cable serves two purposes: first, to carry the traditional analog TV signals, and, second to power the ONUs. See Fig. 5.3 for an illustration of the FTTC architecture. The aspect of power is essential, especially if telephony is carried over the network. The requirements for the system in terms of QoS availability becomes critical, when the service is of a life savingtype, such as telephony. This service must be available in the case of a power outage.

Each ONU is connected in a star structure to relatively few homes—typically between 4 and 16, but in some cases up to 128 or 256 (i.e., each of these homes has its own dedicated cable to the ONU). The distance between the home and the ONU is normally in the range of 50–100 meters, up to approximately 300 meters. The media can be twisted pair copper, or coaxial cable. Different modulation methods are

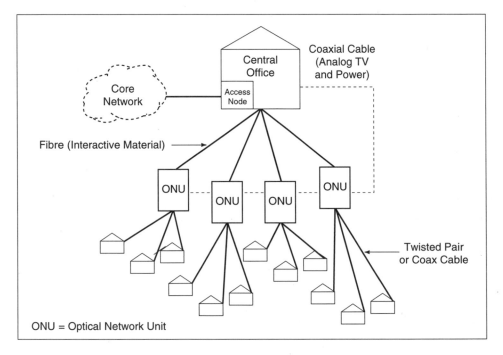

Figure 5.3: Fiber To The Curb access network structure.

used to provide relatively high bandwidth in an asymmetrical fashion. The approach outlined in the DAVIC specification version. 1.0 for instance, describes a scenario with special encapsulated ATM cells modulated with 16-CAP to achieve from 12.96 up to 51.84 Mbps in the downstream direction, and 1.62 up to 19.44 Mbps in the upstream direction via QPSK modulation.

The framing of the ATM cells in the access network includes among other things, a forward error correction field, based on the Reed-Solomon method, to improve the error resilience. Other techniques to improve the error resilience and transmission quality include convolutional interleaving and randomization of the bitstream. The convolutional interleaving "shuffles" the bytes, so that possible error bursts are spread over more frames. It is thereby more likely that the Reed-Solomon algorithms can correct the errors, as the number of errors per frame is lower. The randomization of the bitstream is done by applying a certain Pseudo Random Bit Sequence (PRBS) repetitively. This makes it possible to send out the signal with a fairly even spectral distribution on the physical level. Note that FTTC is known also as Switched Digital Video (SVD).

5.3.3 ADSL/VDSL

To carry VoD services, the ADSL technology uses the existing twisted pair copper cable infrastructure, which is currently used mainly for telephone communication. This is achieved by applying different modulation schemes, such as Carrierless Amplitude Modulation (CAP) or Discrete Multitone (DMT), to achieve the higher throughput. See Fig. 5.4. The infrastructure can realistically only carry one MPEG-2 compressed digital video program at a time, due to the 6 Mbps that is the upper limit in terms of downstream bandwidth. That means that if the user desires to switch channel, this will physically take place at the central office, rather than in the set top box. The logical choice is therefore to use ADSL for VoD and interactive data transfer applications like Internet access, rather than broadcast services.

Different variants of ADSL have been defined: ADSL-1, ADSL-2 and ADSL-3. The three variants are different in speed, as well as the distance they can cover.

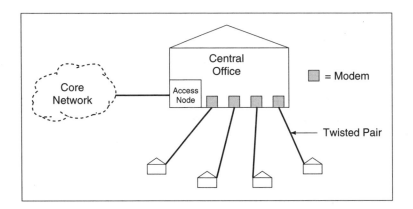

Figure 5.4: The ADSL access network structure.

- ADSL-1 can carry 1.5 Mbps in the downstream direction, and 16 Kbps in the upstream direction, typically over distances of up to 6 km.

- ADSL-2 can carry 3.2 Mbps in the downstream direction and 64 Kbps in the upstream direction, typically over distances of up to 4 km.

- ADSL-3 can carry 6.3 Mbps in the downstream direction and 64 Kbps in the upstream direction, typically over distances of up to 4 km.

In addition to this, the cable can carry information for voice and narrowband ISDN information, yielding a total throughput of approximately 7.2 Mbps in the downstream direction and 642 Kbps in the upstream direction for ADSL-3. The different information flows are placed in different parts of the frequency spectrum, which the twisted pair cable carries. Typically, the downstream digital information, such as compressed digital video, can be carried in the upper part of the spectrum (which normally ranges from 0 to 420 KHz), whereas the upstream information can occupy the middle part, and finally the voice/ISDN part can occupy the lower part. More detailed information on ADSL can be found in ANSI T1.413.

A technology that is quite similar to ADSL is the VDSL. VDSL is, however, capable of carrying higher bandwidth from 10 possibly up to approximately 50 Mbps, but over shorter distances—typically from a few hundred to approximately 1500 meters.

5.3.4 HFC

The HFC access network structure is in many aspects quite similar to the FTTC structure, even though the optical fiber does not go quite as close to the end user. The compressed digital video/interactive material is carried via fiber from the central office to the Optical Network Units/pedestals, which are also fed with the analog signal/power via a coaxial cable. The HFC structure uses a shared media topology from the ONU to the end user, in contrast to the star topology used in FTTC, as shown in Fig. 5.3 on page 226. The coaxial cable between the ONU and the end user, serves a neighborhood—normally in the range of a few hundred households. See Fig. 5.5. A potential problem with HFC is that all noise in the shared media network is concentrated at the ONU—this can become a problem when implementing the return channel for upstream communication.

The approach outlined in the DAVIC specification version 1.0, for instance, outlines a scenario where the coaxial cable, which typically is a few kilometers long, carries analog PAL or NTSC signals in the

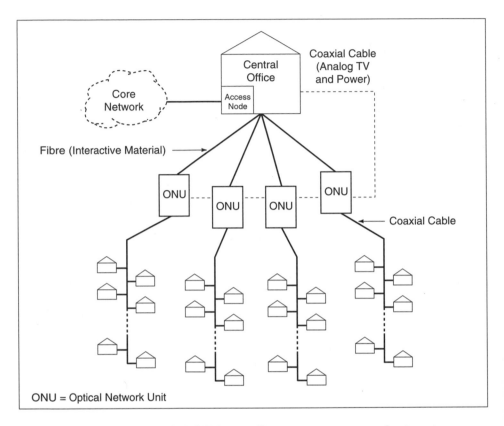

Figure 5.5: The Hybrid Fiber—Coax access network structure.

baseband, as well as the QAM modulated digital video signals in the downstream. In the upstream channel direction, QPSK modulated information from the users are carried back to the ONU/central office. The topology in which the coaxial cable is arranged is the shared media type. To avoid collisions when more people try to use the same resources, and to allow fair access in the return channel direction, a Media Access

Control (MAC) protocol is used similar to what seen in Ethernet LANs. Techniques to improve the error resilience are implemented in a fashion similar as to that seen in the FTTC structure.

5.3.5 FTTH

The FTTH structure is considered as the ultimate solution as it can provide the highest bandwidth to the user compared with other access network technologies. It is, however, also the one that is likely to take the longest time to implement due simply to the relatively high implementation cost, and the fact that most homes are presently connected by either twisted pair copper or coaxial cables (or both)—not with fiber.

FTTH implementations typically have small groups of homes connected directly via fiber in the downstream direction. At some point from the central office, the fiber is split to reach individual homes. A scenario with a 622 Mbps connection being time division multiplexed into four 155 Mbps connections can be seen as an example. At the customers premises, the NT would typically need to perform an optical/electrical conversion before the signals reach the set top box. There are still some open points on how the upstream architecture should be made, as well as how the ONU/splitter should be powered. See Fig. 5.6.

5.3.6 Satellite and Terrestrial Distribution

Satellite broadcasting has been used for distribution of analog video for quite some time. Satellites are very well suited to cover very large geographic areas, typically areas with a diameter of thousands of kilometers.

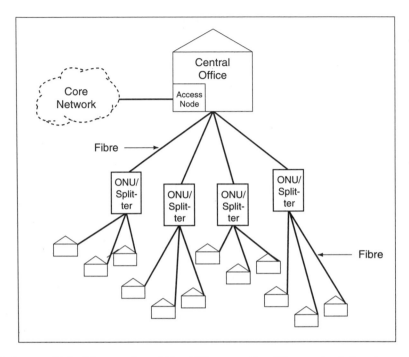

Figure 5.6: Example of the Fiber to the Home Architecture.

Satellites can be used to carry MPEG compressed signals as well. The downstream signal from the core network (ATM-based or non-ATM-based) is transmitted via an uplink, typically using QPSK modulation along with various mechanisms increasing the error resilience, such as convolution and a Reed-Solomon-based FEC. The satellites are operating in the GHz area, and a typical channel can carry about 38 Mbps of useful data, enough to carry 5-8 compressed video channels of normal broadcast quality, along with the accompanying audio channels, tables, etc. For an example of this type of network, the ETSI ETS 300-421 (DVB-S) can be studied.

Satellites were made with the broadcast application in mind, so to allow the satellites to carry information for interactive applications, some sort of upstream channel has to be implemented. This has not yet been well specified, but one possible approach is to implement the return channel via the existing POTS or N-ISDN lines. See Fig. 5-7 for an example of this.

Terrestrial broadcasting has also been used for considerable time for the purpose of analog video distribution, buy with a coverage somewhat smaller than we se with satellite networks. Terrestrial transmission typically covers an area of about 100 kilometers in diameter per transmitter—depending on geography.

Different approaches have been taken on the question of how to make the terrestrial network carry digital video. The DVB-T specification is one example. Terrestrial broadcasting uses the VHF and UHF part of the spectrum (from about 40 MHz to about 800 MHz) and each channel takes 8 MHz (in Europe) or 6 MHz (in the USA). Whereas the analog terrestrial distribution uses mainly AM and FM modulation, transmission of digital TV involves other modulation techniques like COFDM, as described in DVB-T. Techniques to increase the error resilience are similar to what is found in DVB-S. More information can be found in ETSI ETS 300-744.

Similar to satellite implementation, terrestrial distribution does not directly address the return channel needed for implementation of interactive services. Although a final solution does not exist, one possibility could be to use the POTS or N-ISDN lines as seen in the satellite and MMDS scenario.

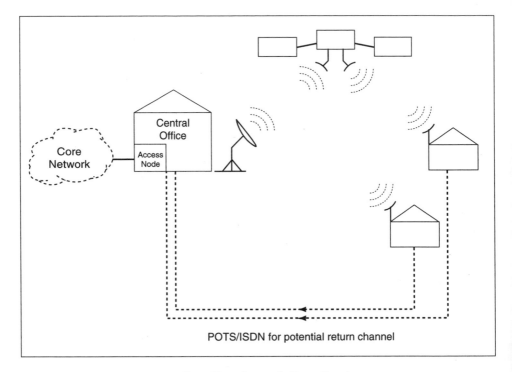

Figure 5.7: Satellite-based distribution system
with POTS/N-ISDN-based return channel.

5.3.7 MMDS / LMDS

MMDS can be seen as a way to get quick access to end users at a relatively low cost. No satellite has to be put in orbit and hardly any cables
have to be laid, hereby making it fasater and less expensive to install
than a complete FTTC or HFC network.

MMDS is based on short range terrestrial broadcasting in the downstream direction. Normally, the frequency band between 2.5 GHz and 2.7 GHz is used, carrying from 100-200 channels of compressed digital video, using different types of modulation, including QAM. Alternatively, up to about 30 channels of analog video can be carried.

The transmitting antenna typically covers a little "cell" of end users within 50 kilometer of the transmitting tower. The users have to be in the line of sight with the transmitter in order to ensure that the microwave signal is conveyed efficiently. This can produce some problems as the quality of the service can be badly affected if physical obstructions block the microwave signal on its way to the end user. In the upstream direction typically the existing POTS/ISDN lines are used to carry the feedback from the interactive users. See Fig. 5.-8.

A similar approach is called Local MDS (LMDS). LMDS covers a much smaller geographical area per transmitter than MMDS, typically only a few kilometers from the base station. Like MMDS, the base station has to be within line of sight with the users. The essential difference to MMDS is that in LMDS not only the downstream but also the upstream information can be carried via the microwave link, that is, no POTS/ISDN lines are used for the upstream. The operating frequency is normally above 10 GHz, and the bandwidth of each channel is 1-2 MHz. The lower frequency bands of the link are typically used for carrying the (differential QPSK modulated) upstream signals, whereas the (QPSK or QAM modulated) downstream signals occupy the upper part of the spectrum.

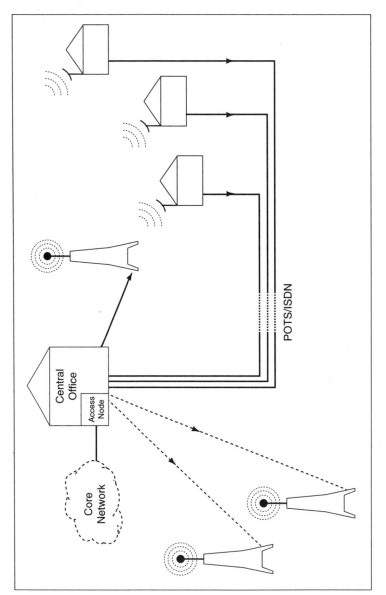

POTS/ISDN

Figure 5.8: MMDS access network structure.

236

5.4 To Get More Details . . .

As access networks are still a subject undergoing much work and a subject where many different approaches to the same general type of access network exist, it is difficult to recommend a single representative piece of literature. A good starting point would be the DAVIC specifications [24], along with the DVB specifications [26, 27, 28]. For ADSL specifically, [49] can be studied. Daniel Minoli's book *Video Dialtone Technology* [55] also gives good background information on some of the technologies behind the access network types.

6

Video in Broadband Networks

6.1 Video in Broadband Networks—On a Page

The previous sections of this book have introduced several technologies, enabling new video based information services. This includes the MPEG technical standards, as well as broadband network technologies, used in both the core and the access networks. However, even if video information is represented digitally in bits and bytes, and the broadband networks have the capacity to carry the video service, there are still many open issues on the actual integration. The applications, such as Video on Demand, require the transmission of video and audio information through a network. Furthermore, a number of additional communication channels are needed between service provider and customer, for instance, to transmit control and management information.

The following section of this book will outline some of the most important approaches that have been taken to handle MPEG video data in broadband networks. The following will be covered:

- The ATM Forum Video on Demand Specification, covering the VoD protocol Reference Model, ATM layer QoS requirements, and AAL-5 mapping.

- ITU-T J.82 transportation of MPEG via AAL-1, covering mapping, Reed-Solomon protection, and interleaving.

- An overview about the efforts of the Internet Engineering Task Force (IETF) to make the Internet ready to deliver real-time services, including video.

- The DAVIC specification, covering the system reference model and the reference points. The architecture and the interfaces of the Service Provider System, Delivery System, and the Service Consumer System will be covered, as well as the S1, S2, S3, S4, and S5 information flow, and the physical layer interface specified by DAVIC.

6.2 Introduction

The previous chapters of this book introduced a number of technologies directly related to the digital video and the networking world. However, the only common denominator is the fact that the data is represented digitally. It is an unresolved question on how exactly both worlds should be brought together. Furthermore, in the near future there will not be a "one and only" single answer to this question. Currently, we can think of a number of services where digital video will be used:

- Cable TV network based services

- Telecommunication network based services

- Digital Broadcast Satellite (DBS), Direct to the Home (DTH) services

- Terrestrial Digital Broadcast services

- Commercial On-line services

- Internet/World Wide Web based services

Looking at this list, one can identify two major trends that the industry is following in order to include digital video in future information services.

One trend is the use of digital video in broadcasting applications. These broadcasting applications are usually based on cable, terrestrial, or satellite distribution methods. Instead of transmitting analog signals, digital data is now transported. The simple broadcast application is getting enhanced by having services like Near Video on Demand (NVoD) or Pay Per View (PPV) installed. Fully Interactive Video on

Demand (IVoD) is still the long term goal. The other trend is to use digital video in information systems that are based on data networks, with the Internet related protocols as the most common delivery mechanism. In this case, the data packets are now not only carrying text and pictures, but also video and audio information.

Table 6.1 shows some of the benefits and drawbacks of the two trends.

	Benefits	Drawbacks
Broadcast approach	• High bandwidth in cable networks • TV set pervasive • Guaranteed down-stream bandwidth	• Interactivity difficult • No technology standard for backchannel • No standard for data services in cable/satellite networks • Different regional/national technical deployments
Datacom/ Internet industry approach	• Standards for interactive communication mature • De-facto standard user-interface (Web) • Internationally deployed	• No standard for data services in cable/satellite networks • Bandwidth currently limited • Quality of services guarantee still a problem • Initially not developed for real-time service like video

Table 6.1: Digital video delivery approaches.

Both trends are, of course, supported by different industry groups, each trying to establish standards and specifications for their own suite of applications. On one side we have the TV broadcasting, cable networks, and satellite industry, which is trying to make digital video (and also data services) a success in their technical infrastructure. On the other side there is the datacom and telecom industry, trying to use and enhance the current information systems with the digital video component.

So, at the time of this writing there is no unique, standard way to include digital video into data or telecom networks. Furthermore, we can see different standard organizations working on the subject. The ATM forum, for example, did some work on how to transport MPEG video data in ATM cells and how ATM forum signalling should be used in a video delivery network. The Internet Engineering Task Force (IETF) started work to define how IP data packets should be transported over cable TV networks and how to transport MPEG data with the IP protocols. In this chapter, we will have a look on the work of the most important activities in this area. We will cover the work done by the Digital Audio Video Council (DAVIC), the ATM forum, the International Telecommunication Union (ITU), and the Internet Engineering Task Force (IETF).

6.3 The ATM Forum Video on Demand Implementation Agreement

6.3.1 Introduction

The ATM forum established a technical sub-committee with the task to work on questions related to Audiovisual Multimedia Services (AMS) on top of ATM. The AMS technical committee started to develop an Implementation Agreement (IA) for a possible Video on Demand application. Version 1.0 of this Implementation Agreement was finalized in late 1995 and covers several aspects of transmitting video or audio data via an ATM-based broadband network.

6.3.2 ATM Forum VoD Protocol Reference Model

The Video on Demand implementation agreement defines a protocol reference model, which covers both the control and the user plane protocol stacks. Fig. 6.1 shows the protocol reference model. Please note that in this reference model, ATM and AAL-5 are the common lower layers for all other protocol stacks.

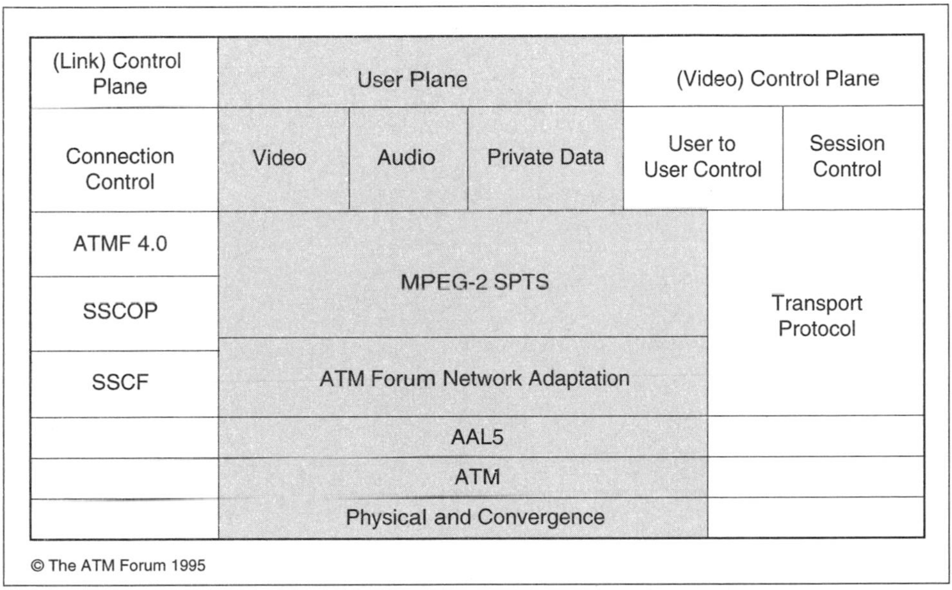

(Link) Control Plane	User Plane			(Video) Control Plane	
Connection Control	Video	Audio	Private Data	User to User Control	Session Control
ATMF 4.0	MPEG-2 SPTS			Transport Protocol	
SSCOP					
SSCF	ATM Forum Network Adaptation				
	AAL5				
	ATM				
	Physical and Convergence				

© The ATM Forum 1995

Figure 6.1: ATM Forum VoD Protocol Reference Model.

6.3.3 Network Adaptation

Possibly the most important part of the ATM forum implementation agreement is the definition of how MPEG-2 transport stream packets are transmitted over ATM. The IA defines AAL-5 as the adaptation layer to be used for the transport of MPEG-2 packets, and it also defines how transport packets are mapped into AAL-5 SDUs[1]. Basically one to n transport packets can be mapped into one AAL-5 SDU. However, the IA defines all equipment that conforms to the IA should at least

---

[1]SDU = Service Data Unit. (Equivalent to payload of a Protocol Data Unit, PDU.)

support the mapping of 2 transport packets into one AAL-5 SDU. The value two is also the default value, if the network uses Permanent Virtual Connections (PVCs). If switched virtual connections (SVCs) are used, the value for n is negotiable.

The IA specifies the following rules for $n = 2$:

- AAL-5 with a "Null" Service Specific Convergence Subayer shall be used.

- An AAL-5 PDU shall contain two TS Packets, unless it contains the last TS Packet of the Single Program Transport Stream.

- An AAL-5 PDU shall contain only one MPEG-2 Transport Packet, if that MPEG-2 Transport Packet is the last Transport Packet of the Single Program Transport Stream.

Figure 6.2 shows the mapping of two transport stream packets in an AAL-5 PDU. Please note that in the case of $n = 2$, the transport packets need 376 bytes, which are mapped together with the CPCS trailer of 8 bytes into the payload of 8 ATM cells.

The mapping process is called PCR-unaware because it does not consider whether or not the transport packets contain a PCR timestamp or not. If the transport packets contains a PCR, the mapping process does not define any special action, such as starting a new AAL-5 PDU. This was under heavy discussion because accessing the PCR value in the MPEG-2 transport packet does now require additional

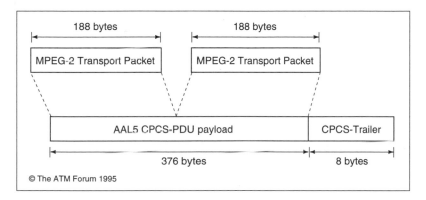

Figure 6.2: Mapping of MPEG-2 transport
packets according to the ATM Forum.

buffering to guarantee constant access delays during PDU reassem-
bling. Please see the annex A of [56] for a discussion of the end-to-end
delay issues.

In the case that a CRC checksum error is detected in the AAL-5
CPCS PDU, but the actual length of the PDU still corresponds to the
length field in the CPCS trailer, it is up to the receiver to discard or not
discard this PDU. If the whole PDU is discarded, it would lead to the
loss of a number of MPEG-2 transport packets. On the other hand, the
bit error might not have a serious impact on the upper layer payload
data. Since MPEG-2 systems provide error indication bits in the
MPEG-2 transport packet header, the occurred error could be indicated here and further action could be done by the MPEG-2 decoder.

6.3.4 Traffic Parameters and Quality of Service Parameters

When an ATM connection is setup to transport the MPEG-2 SPTS data, a set of traffic and quality of service parameters have to be specified. This is done by the broadband network signalling protocols, as described in Chapter 4. Some of the parameters are a negotiable at connection setup time, but some have to be specified within the scope of the traffic contract. For a VCC that is carrying MPEG-2 data, the following QoS parameters have to be specified:

- Cell Delay Variation—tolerance and peak-to-peak value
- Cell Transfer Delay—maximum value
- Cell Loss Ratio (CLR)
- Cell Error Ratio (CER)
- Severely Errored Cell Block Ratio (SECBR)

The meaning of these parameters is outlined in Section 4.5.9, and specified in ITU-T I.356 and the ATM Forum UNI specifications.

6.4 ITU-T Recommendation J.82

Mapping of MPEG-2 in AAL-1

Also in the ITU, the method of encapsulating MPEG TSPs in ATM cells has recieved much attention. The reccommendation J.82 describes the method using AAL-5 as outlined above. In addition, J.82 describes an alternative method using AAL-1 as the encapsulation. The technique using AAL-1 is more complex, but can, on the other hand, offer more protection against ATM layer impairments, if this is needed.

As the quality of the video service can be influenced drastically by the various ATM layer impairments, significant efforts have been put in to specifying mechanisms that can deal with these problems. One possible solution is to use the AAL-1, in combination with certain error correction schemes. The use of AAL-1 brings a solution to the problem of jitter in the network, by means of the time stamp carried in the CSI field of the SAR PDU. Via this timestamp, it is possible to emulate a constant end-to-end delay scenario. In practice, it has to be done by implementing buffering circuits in the network elements, such as the switches in order to smooth out the cell delay variation throughout the network. The AAL-1 format furthermore addresses the problem of cell loss and cell misinsertion, as problems can be identified by means of the sequence counter, also present in the SAR PDU. The aspects of error correction and recovery of lost cells must however also be addressed for transmission of MPEG-2 compressed digital video. The mechanisms for achieving this have therefore been included in the part of the AAL specification, I.363, that deals with AAL-1.

ITU-T recommendation J.82 outlines the use of AAL-1 (as well as AAL-5, as mentioned above) for constant bit rate video transmission in the B-ISDN. It describes the usage of AAL-1, in combination with a FEC (Forward Error Correction) scheme, based on the RS (Reed Solomon) technique, combined with byte interleaving.

The forward error correction is done over a group of ATM cells. Specifically, 31 188 byte transport stream packets are organized horizontally into 47 rows of 124 bytes in a matrix, as shown in Fig. 6.3. Via this interleaving process, a certain protection against large bursts of errors is obtained, as the bursts are "spread" out over more data, making it easier for the FEC mechanism to handle. This structure is then protected by the Reed-Solomon technique (124,128), and four 47 byte columns of FEC information are added. The structure is now equal to the AAL-1 CS PDU. The CS PDU is transmitted column by column, via 128 AAL-1 SAR PDUs. The beginning of a new CS PDU can be identified via the CSI field in the AAL-1 SAR PDU.

The effects of using this error protection are that out of the group of 128 cells, the loss of up to 4 cells can be corrected. Furthermore, up to 2 erred bytes out of 128 bytes can be corrected.

6.4.2 Mapping of MPEG-2 in AAL-5

The part of ITU-T J.82 that is focusing on AAL-5 follows the ATM Forum IA for VoD, which is described in Section 6.3.

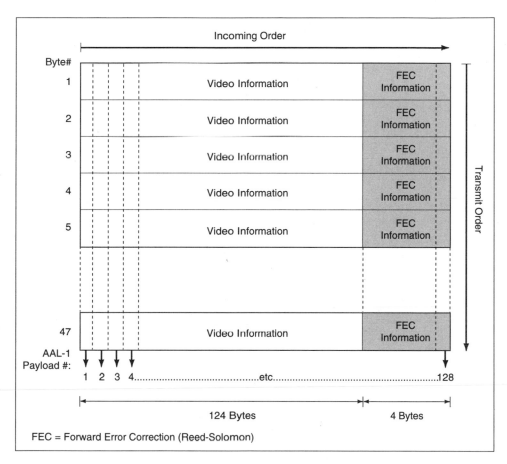

Figure 6.3: Structure of video and FEC information
in the interleaving matrix, used with AAL-1.

6.5 Internet Engineering Task Force (IETF) Work Groups: Digital Video in the Internet

6.5.1 Introduction

The network concepts described before, namely ATM and the B-ISDN, are not the only networking technologies considered to carry video data traffic. The World Wide Web application on the Internet can be seen as probably the most desired service for residential multimedia systems' architectures. A big advantage of the web application is the fact that the World Wide Web does not present the extreme bandwidth requirements, as a video entertainment service.

However, the demand for video as an additional information type in the World Wide Web is certainly present. This demand resulted in a couple of activities to make the current Internet protocol environment suitable to carry real-time traffic like video and audio. Since the work in this area is presently progressing, this section will give only a very brief introduction into the relevant issues.

The are basically two major problems if one think about video in the Internet. The first issue is once again the question on how to deliver the necessary bandwidth to the end users. The access technologies, which were explained in Chapter 5, will provide different solutions for this problem. The second issue is related to the current Internet service model and the datacommunication protocols that are used in the Internet. The quality of service requirements, which video data demands from the network and which were described in Section 4.5.9, are also very valid if the Internet is used as delivery mechanism. Unfortunately, these requirements are in contradiction to the design of the current Internet protocols and its service model.

6.5.2 The Internet Service Model

To make the Internet capable to support video services, some fundamental changes in the Internet service model have to be considered. Currently, the Internet is based on a best-effort and point-to-point data delivery. In other words, there is no guarantee that a packet sent out will reach its destination. Assuming that it will be successfully delivered, it is unknown before hand how long this will take. Also, it is not clear how long it will take for the next packet to reach its destination because this packet could take a different path in the network. The equipment and protocols currently used in the Internet are working in "best-effort" mode to deliver each packet and treat each packet in the same way. This approach is quite sufficient for most of the application using the Internet today. However, with the advent of the World Wide Web, this best-effort concept is pushed to its limits. The amount of participants in the network has increased (both on the client and the server side) and the content to be transmitted is getting more and more bandwidth consuming. For the Internet, this results in the fact that the bandwidth is getting shared between more and more applications and users. Because of this, we are getting totally different results in accessing the same server in the Internet at different times of the day or different days of the week. With applications like Web-surfing or file transfer, this might be still tolerable. However, a service that includes streamed-video simply does not work if a certain set of requirements are not fulfilled by the network. Of course, we could think about adapting the quality of the video according to the provided network quality, such as decreasing the temporal or spatial resolution of the video pictures. However, there are some limits to this given by the human perception, as explained in Chapter 2.

To get around these problems, a new service model for the Internet is needed. This service model has to be able to support integrated services (IS), including real-time data like video or audio. The core of this new service model is the support of a guaranteed Quality of Service (QoS) level for an application. There are basically two methods to guarantee Quality of Service :

- Provide more bandwidth if needed: This implies that at every point of the video data end-to-end route, enough bandwidth is available to cope with new additional data traffic. In other words, bandwidth would become an infinite resource. If we think about technologies like Wavelength Division Multiplexing (WDM) this might become reality for parts of the Internet backbone network in the mid-term future. Some other parts, on the other hand, might not be realized with this technology and therefore become a limiting factor. This is especially true for access network technologies, mentioned in Chapter 5. However, it is almost certain that additional bandwidth has to be paid, and this of course could become a limiting factor as well.

- Reserve resources upfront: With a knowledge about the maximum tolerable impairment boundaries, it should be possible to reserve a certain amount of resources in the network to guarantee the reliable and timely delivery of data packets within these boundaries. This approach is currently pursued in the Internet community with the development of the Resource Reservation Protocol (RSVP). The B-ISDN network model also uses resource reservation. It is taking place during the connection setup phase, where QoS parameters are negogiated.

Another issue with the Internet concept in regards to video distribution is the usage of point-to-point connections. If a server in the Internet sends data to a number of different clients, separate data packets for each client are sent, even if the content of the data packets is the same and the route they are traveling is mostly the same. If we think about a video broadcasting application, this implies that the server would send the same pictures for every client. The bandwidth requirements for the network link between the server and the network would therefore be quite high.

A different approach is realized by using multicast to transmit the data. In the case of multicasting, the server would transmit the data only to a address and the network would take care of distributing it to the clients belonging to this multicast address. An experimental multicast system is established on the Internet and is used for the video distribution of IETF events.

6.5.3 IETF Work Groups
and Standards

The issues of resource reservation, multicasting, and real-time services in the Internet are being addressed by the IETF in different work groups. Multicasting will become a feature of the next Internet protocol IPv6. Resource reservation is addressed by the work that is done on the RSVP protocol.

Another important protocol that might play a very important role in order to establish real-time services in the Internet is the Real-Time-Protocol (RTP). As we saw in Chapter 4, MPEG-2 also covers time synchronization issues in the MPEG-2 Systems part. However, there are other digital video formats that do not include this functionality, such as M-JEPG. To make it possible to transmit those formats via the Internet, a protocol was needed that provides the necessary support for data streams with timing properties. RTP was developed to do just this. The actual RTP specification (RFC 1889) is quite generic. In order to use it with a digital video format, such as MPEG, an additional profile and payload format specification is needed. For MPEG coded video these specification are defined with RFC 1890 and RFC 2038. As said before, the RTP protocol can take over some of the functionality of MPEG-2 Systems (in regard to time synchronization) and therefore the RTP payload format for MPEG coded video foresees the use of MPEG audio and video elementary streams mapped directly into RTP packets. Table 6.2 summarizes the ITEF standardization activities related to the delivery of real-time services on the Internet.

Integrated Services Model Issue	Protocol	RFC	IETF working group
Multicast	IP Version 6	RFC 1883	IP next generation (ipng)
Resource Reservation	RSVP	Internet Draft [37]	Resource Reservation Setup Protocol (rsvp)
Real-time traffic	RTP	RFC 1889, RFC1890, RFC 2038	Audio-Video Transport (avt)

Table 6.2: Issues related to digital video in the Internet.

Once the standards in Table 6.2 have been finalized and are implemented by router and other network equipment, a video application scenario in the Internet could look like the one shown in Fig. 6.4 on page 258.

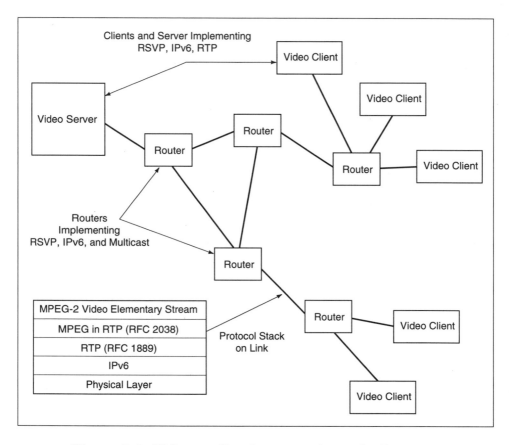

Figure 6.4: Video application scenario on the Internet.

6.6 The Digital Audio-Visual Council (DAVIC) Association Specification

6.6.1 Introduction

By finalizing the ATM Forum VoD Implementation Agreement and the ITU J.82 recommendation, the first steps were taken to define how digital video data should be transported in ATM networks. Beside these specifications, more building blocks like B-ISDN signalling protocols (Q.2931) or video application session signalling (MPEG-2 DSM-CC) were developed. But even with these essential building blocks for new multimedia services becoming well defined, specifications on how all these blocks should work together were still missing.

To make the new services a reality, all the mentioned "building blocks" needed to be integrated into a complete system. This integration is best supported by having a kind of reference model in place, which describes where all the different blocks should fit in.

A reference model describes well-defined entities belonging to the system and it also describes interfaces between these entities. Furthermore, the information flows between the entities have to be well defined. Having such a reference model in place, equipment interoperability would improve and the development of new services and applications would be accelerated.

The Digital Audio-Visual Council (DAVIC) was founded with exactly this purpose in mind. (See Fig. 6.5). None of the other standardization groups, like ISO/IEC-MPEG, ATM Forum, or ITU, focused directly on the task of developing an overall reference model supporting new digital audio and video-based applications and services. DAVIC was founded in 1994 and its memberlist includes all major computer vendors, service providers, and video equipment manufacturers. As said in the introduction of this chapter, there are currently different trends in the industry trying to bring multimedia services to the home. DAVIC tries to address both approaches, by recently including Internet access and Internet real-time services in its scope of work.

DAVIC published its first specification (Version 1.0) at the end of 1995. The structure of the specification is driven by the envisioned applications, which are assumed to be designed according to DAVIC specifications. Because of this, the DAVIC specification describes common (core) functionalities and requirements, which are almost certain to be used by multimedia applications. For instance, there must be a group of functions dealing with the transport of data between service provider and end-user. Also, some functions are required to control the application session and the application itself. Please see Fig. 6.6 for the different function groups DAVIC defines. Fig. 6.6 also shows the common generic application requirements foreseen by the DAVIC group. Besides the specification of the core functionality and the common application requirements, DAVIC describes in some detail examples for the most common multimedia applications:

- Movies on Demand
- Teleshopping

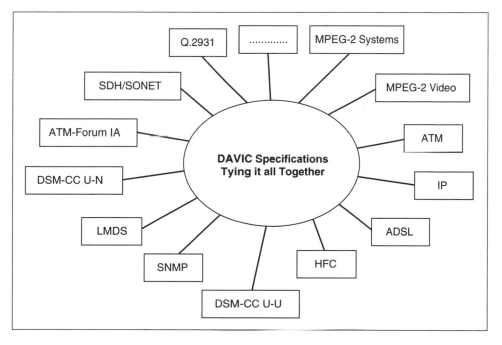

Figure 6.5: DAVIC Scope.

- Broadcast
- Near Video on Demand
- Delayed Broadcast
- Games
- Telework
- Karaoke on Demand
- Internet Access

Generic Requirements of Applications and Services	Example Applications	
Navigation and Interaction Service and Content Management General Aspects on Environment Security	Movies on Demand Teleshopping Broadcast Near Video on Demand Delayed Broadcast	Games Telework Karaoke on Demand News on Demand Internet Access

Function Groups				
User Profile	Usage Data	Navigation & Selection	Access Control	Media Synchronisation
User Profile	Presentation Control	Bit Transport	Application Control	Session

Reference Models, Architectures, Technologies and Tools						
System Reference Model	Service Provider System Architecture	Service Consumer System Architecture	Delivery System Architecture	Protocols and Physical Interfaces	Information Representation	Dynamic Flows

Figure 6.6: Parts of the DAVIC specification.

For each of these applications, DAVIC specifies the different functions that the end-user could use or the service provider or network provider has to offer. After the definition of the core functionality and applications, the major part of the DAVIC specification is then describing which technology and tools should be used to realize the above mentioned functionalities. (See Fig. 6.6)

A very essential part of the DAVIC specification is the description of the system reference model, where all the different entities belonging to a multimedia system are defined. Furthermore, well-defined interface points between these different entities are introduced. This system reference model is described in more detail in Section 6.6.2. DAVIC refines the service provider system, the service consumer system and the delivery system to some detail, introducing internal reference architectures and reference points for each of them. From a network technology point of view, the parts dealing with the delivery system, architecture and the protocols are the most interesting. The delivery system architecture and interfaces will be explained in more detail in section 6.6.3. The protocol part of the DAVIC specification lists the protocols and physical layer technologies that should be used at the different interfaces of a DAVIC systems' reference model. DAVIC considers these technologies as tools, which can be combined in order to create a system supporting the intended application. DAVIC mostly utilizes existing standards (e.g., the ones made by the ATM forum, MPEG, or the ITU), but also introduces new concepts based on member proposals. Section 6.6.4 will give an overview about the protocols stacks used in the DAVIC specification.

The Information Representation part of the DAVIC specification defines which technology is used for what kind of monomedia (e.g., ISO/IEC 13818-1 MPEG-2 video for the compressed video information type or HTML 2.0 for the text information type).

The dynamic flows part of the specification finally puts the defined information flows (see Section 6.6.4) into a relation. The set-up and tear-town of video application sessions and the service transfer between servers are described in detail. In this context, DAVIC also considers different physical implementation scenarios, like ATM to the end-user or ATM termination in the access network. It would go beyond the scope of this book to present more detail here, and we would like to refer to the actual DAVIC specifications for a complete coverage.

6.6.2 DAVIC System Reference Model

The typical DAVIC System Reference Model (DSRM) consists of four main blocks. The Content Provider System (CPS), the Service Provider System (SPS), the Service Consumer System (SCS), and the Delivery System (DS). In the real world, the CPS could be a server system of some Hollywood studio providing different movies or TV programs to be downloaded into some service provider system. This service provider system could belong to a cable TV company, which is offering a video on demand service. The service consumer system would then be a simple set top box to decode the incoming video data. The delivery systems are basically the networks connecting the provider systems and the consumer system. Different versions of the DS might be used for the communication between the CPS and the SPS on one side, and the SPS and the SCS on the other side. In the case of the DS between the service provider and the consumer, the network could be a HFC access network combined with an ATM core network. Between the content provider and the service provider, there may be a fiber-based ATM network, since both business organizations might have fiber to the building (FTTB) deployed.

The information that is exchanged between the different systems can be subdivided into the content information and the control information. The DAVIC system reference model currently defines five information flows, labeled S1 to S5, where only the S1 flow is used for content information. The five information flows are described in more detail in Section 6.4.4. Fig. 6.7 shows the DAVIC system reference model.

Furthermore, the DAVIC model provides well defined interfaces, called reference points. Reference points exist between the high-level

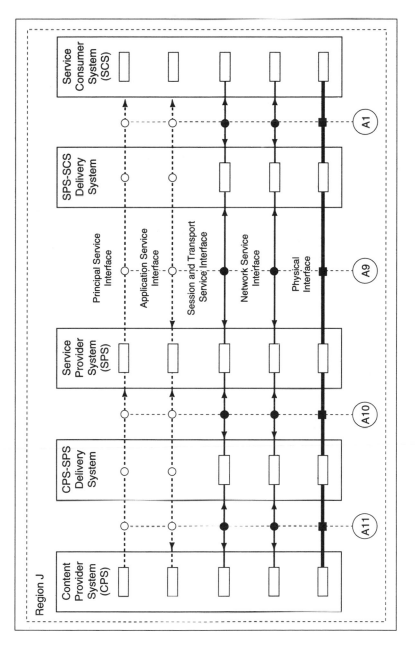

Figure 6.7: DAVIC system reference model.

systems, but also between entities within these systems. The reference points are labeled A0 to A11 and are shown in Table 6.3.

According to DAVIC, the reference model exists in one specific geographic region and can be combined with other models in other regions.

Reference Point	Description
A0 (internal to STB)	Interface between Network Interface, and other compnents of a STU. The reference model for a set top unit foresees the functional block of a Network Interface Unit and an application processing part with the A0 interface inbetween.
A1, A1*, A1:	The interface between the service consumer system and the SPS-SCS delivery system. This interface would be used to connect the set top unit to the access network connection (e.g., an ADSL modem). A1*: The interface between an enhanced in-house network and the STU.
A2, A3, A4, A5, A6, A7, A8 (internal to DS)	Internal interfaces of the delivery system. A2 and A3 are interfaces between equipment belonging to the access-network, A5 to A8 are network internal interfaces for control and management. The A4 interface connects the core network and the access network.
A9	The interface between the service provider system and the SPS-SCS delivery system. In the case of an interactive video on demand server, this could be a SONET/SDH-based ATM link.
A10	The interface between the service provider system, and the CPS—SPS delivery system.
A11	The interface between the content provider system, and the CPS—SPS delivery system.

Table 6.3: DAVIC reference points.

6.6.3 DAVIC Delivery System

The task of the delivery system in the DAVIC reference model is to connect the content provider via the service provider to the consumer and to route the different information flows. To do this, the delivery system uses different network technologies, which can be divided into wire-based and wireless networks. In the case of wired or cabled networks, the delivery system can be refined into several components like the core network, the access network, and eventually the customer premise network. Fig. 6.8 on page 268 shows the structure of a wired-based delivery system according to DAVIC 1.0.

The core network is used to deliver information flows from the service provider to a certain point (reference point A4) from which the distribution of the information to the consumer is taken over by the access network. The core network is therefore designed to carry huge amounts of information, with reasonably high speed. In the core network, DAVIC assumes the use of ATM. The access network is designed to connect the end user in a cost effective way, so that shared access methods or the resuse of existing cabling infrastructure (e.g., cable TV or telephony networks) is desired.

6.6.4 The DAVIC Information Flows

DAVIC currently defines five types of information flows traversing a delivery system. One flow carries the content, the other four flows are used for control and management of the content flow and of the

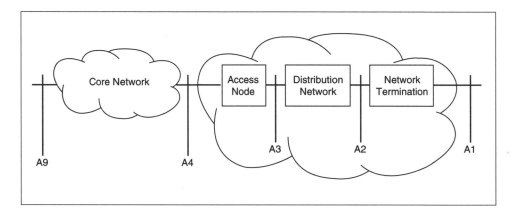

Figure 6.8: DAVIC delivery system.

equipment belonging to the different DAVIC systems. In the following section these information flows will be described with focus on used protocols. Please see Table 6.4 for an overview of the DAVIC flows.

The different entities in the DAVIC system reference model (e.g., the service provider system, the delivery system, and the service consumer systems) have to implement the processing of the different flows in hard- and software. Fig. 6.9 on page 270 shows that the S1 and S2 flows are only processed by the server provider and the server consumer system, but S3 and S4 are also processed in the delivery system.

S1 Flow: Content Flow

As stated, the S1 flow carries the actual content of a service (e.g., an MPEG coded movie). Depending of the network technology, the MPEG

DAVIC Flow	Description
S1	Content flow, consumed by the user (e.g., a movie).
S2	Application control flow, carrying an application signalling protocol altering the behavior of the content flow.
S3	Session control flow, carrying a session control protocol, typically altering the behavoir/state of equipment in the SPS and SCS.
S4	Link control flow, carrying a network signalling protocol, typically altering the behavoir/state of equipment in the SPS and SCS.
S5	Management flow, carrying a network management protocol.

Table 6.4: DAVIC information flows.

protocol stack is transmitted on top of ATM, or directly on top of the physical and convergence layer. The latter is used in the case of satellite transmission systems, or access network technologies, which are not supporting ATM. In this case, the multiplexing of different programs becomes a function of the MPEG-2 transport layer, while in the case of ATM, the virtual channels connections can be used for the multiplexing of programs. The S1 flow protocol architecture for an ATM based network is summarized in Fig. 6.10 on page 271.

269

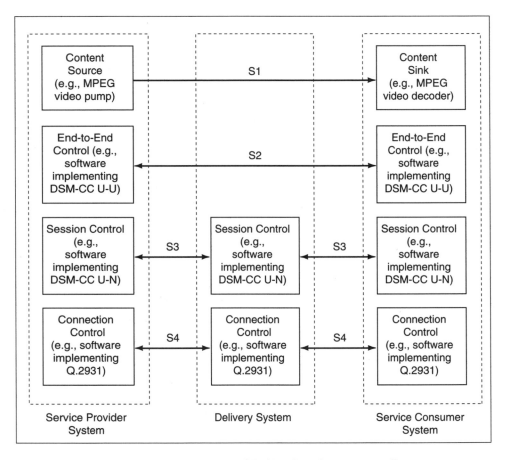

Figure 6.9: Processing of DAVIC information flows.

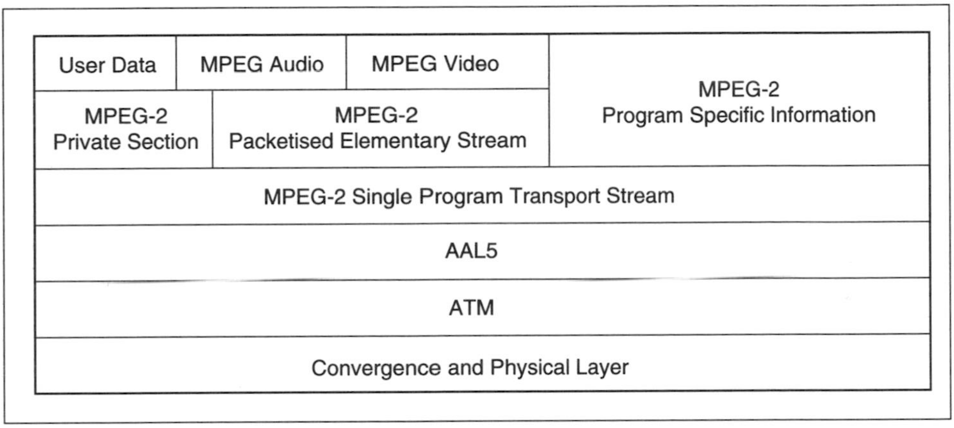

User Data	MPEG Audio	MPEG Video	MPEG-2 Program Specific Information
MPEG-2 Private Section	MPEG-2 Packetised Elementary Stream		
MPEG-2 Single Program Transport Stream			
AAL5			
ATM			
Convergence and Physical Layer			

Figure 6.10: S1 protocol stack.

S2 Flow: Control Flow

The S2 flow is related to the S1 flow, but is used as the control channel for the service content. The best way to illustrate the use of the S2 is a movie on demand application, where the S2 flow is used to transmit VCR equivalent commands like fast forward, rewind, and pause. DAVIC defines DSM-CC user-user signaling as the protocol to be used for S2. DSM-CC user-user is based on TCP/IP, illustrated in Fig. 6.11.

S3 Flow: Control Flow

The S3 flow is used to configure and control application sessions between a server and client. Following the example of a movie on demand application, the S3 flow would be used to create the S1 and S2 connection between the client and the server. DAVIC again refers to

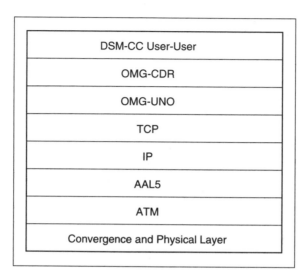

Figure 6.11: S2 protocol stack.

MPEG-2 DSM-CC to be used as the communication standard for S3. However, in this case, it is the user-network part of DSM-CC. In Fig. 6.12, the protocols stack used for S3 is illustrated.

The DAVIC 1.0 specification only uses a subset of the command sequences defined in the DSM-CC user-to-network specification. The DSM-CC specification defines a scenario where the server initiates a connection to the client. In DAVIC 1.0, this scenario is not foreseen, so that DAVIC only uses a subset of the DSM-CC command sequences, DSM-CC messages and resource descriptors.

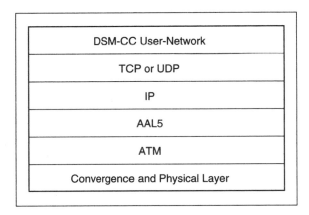

| DSM-CC User-Network |
| TCP or UDP |
| IP |
| AAL5 |
| ATM |
| Convergence and Physical Layer |

Figure 6.12: S3 protocol stack.

S4 Flow: Control Flow

The S4 flow is the network layer connection control between client and server. It is used to setup and release connection between the server (or client) and the delivery system. DAVIC specifies that B-ISDN signaling, which was described in detail in Section 4.5.11 should be used for this task. It only specifies the ITU-T variant to be used. The ATM forum signaling variants are not considered in the DAVIC 1.0 specification. Please note that for the S4 flow, DAVIC 1.0 always deals with the communication between terminal equipment and network, and is therefore not considering the NNI signaling protocols.

As for the S3 flows and DSM-CC, only a subset of the of the ITU-T recommendation Q.2931 is supported within the S4 flow. This is true for the defined messages, messages flows, and information elements. For instance, the DAVIC 1.0 only uses point-to-point connections and is not considering point-to-multipoint setups. See Fig. 6.13.

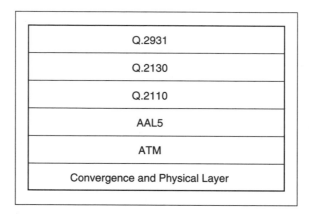

Figure 6.13: S4 protocol stack.

S5 Flow: Management Flow

The S5 flow is used for the network and system management. DAVIC considers both SNMP and the ITU-T recommended CMIP to be used for these functions. SNMP should be used to access the STB and server MIB; CMIP should be used for the delivery system components. DAVIC 1.0 currently defines an MIB for STU, which is part of the DAVIC 1.0 specification. For the service provider system, the MIB-2 is defined to be used. Fig. 6.14 summarizes the protocols to be used for the network management of an network element, which is ATM capable. In the case that the system does not support ATM, Ethernet or HDLC can be used as lower layers.

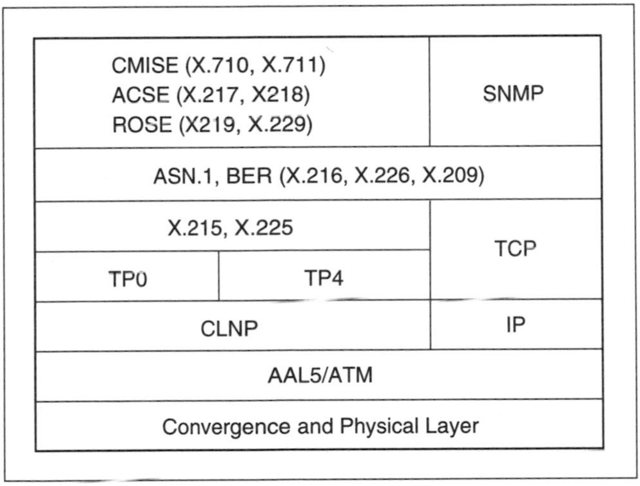

CMISE (X.710, X.711) ACSE (X.217, X218) ROSE (X219, X.229)		SNMP
ASN.1, BER (X.216, X.226, X.209)		
X.215, X.225		TCP
TP0	TP4	
CLNP		IP
AAL5/ATM		
Convergence and Physical Layer		

Figure 6.14: S5 protocol stack.

Physical Layers in the DAVIC Delivery System

The physical layers that are currently defined to be used in the delivery system are shown in Table 6.5. Depending on the part of the delivery system that the flow is traversing, the physical layer might change. For instance, the S1 flow might use the SONET/SDH physical layer in the core network, but in the access network the SDH/SONET layer is replaced with the physical layer of a FTTC implementation.

Core Network Physical Layer	Bit Rate	Access Network Physical Layer	Bit Rate
SDH STM-1	155.52 Mbit/s	PSTN	max. 28.8 kbit/s
SDH STM-4	622.08 Mbit/s	ISDN	2 x 64 kbit/s
SONET OC-3c	155.52 Mbit/s	ADSL	max. 7 Mbit/s downstream max. 640 kbit/s upstream
SONET OC-12	622.08 Mbit/s	FTTC	up to 50 Mbit/s downstream 1.62–19.44 Mbit/s upstream
PDH J2	6.312 Mbit/s	HFC (QAM)	between 19–51 Mbit/s downstream
PDH E3	34.368 Mbit/s	HFC (QPSK)	1.544 Mbit/s downstream 256 kbit/s or 1.544 Mbit/s upstream
PDH DS-3	44.736 Mbit/s	ATM Forum	25.6 Mbit/s
PDH E4	139.264 Mbit/s		

Table 6.5: DAVIC physical layers and corresponding bitrates.

6.7 To Get More Details . . .

To learn more about the mapping of MPEG coded video into ATM cells, the ITU [51] and the ATM Forum standards [56] have to be considered. The ATM forum document has a number of informative annexes discussing end-to-end delay variation issues. The Internet related work has very good coverage on the World Wide Web at the IETF homepage at http://www.ietf.org. This is a good starting point to get the RFCs [43–47] and Internet drafts (e.g., [36]), describing the state-of-the art of digital video on the Internet. To learn more about the DAVIC reference models and tools, the actual DAVIC specifications [23] are the best source. Some parts are presented in the form of a technical report and very easy to read. DAVIC also has a home page at http://www.davic.org

List of References

[1] Hewlett-Packard. *1996 Digital Video Test Symposium—Attendee Handbook.*

[2] Balabanian, V.; Casey, L.; Greene, N.; and Adams, C. "An Introduction to Digital Storage Media—Command and Control," *IEEE Communications Magazine,* Vol. 34, No. 11 (November 1996).

[3] Prycker, de Martin. *Asynchronous Transfer Mode,* Prentice Hall: Upper Saddle River, NJ, 1995.

[4] ITU-T. *ATM Cell Mapping into Plesiochronous Digital Hierarchy (PDH).* ITU-T Rec. G.804, 1993.

[5] Händel, R.; Huber, M.N.; and Schröder, S. *ATM Networks, Concepts, Protocols, and Applications.* Addison-Wesley: Reading, MA, 1994.

[6] ATM Forum. *ATM User-Network Interface Specification 3.0, 1993.*

[7] ATM Forum. *ATM User-Network Interface Specification 3.1, 1994.*

[8] Tsutsui, K.; Suzuki, H.; Shimoyoshi, O.; Sonohara, M.; Akagiri, K.; and Heddle, R.M. *ATRAC: Adaptive Transform Acoustic Coding*

for MiniDisc. Audio Engineering Society, Reprint from 93rd convention in San Francisco, October 1-4, 1992.

[9] ITU-T. *B-ISDN Asynchronous Transfer Mode Functional Characteristics.* ITU-T Rec. I.150, 1995.

[10] ITU-T. *B-ISDN ATM Adaptation Layer (AAL) Functional Description.* ITU-T Rec. I.362, 1993.

[11 ITU-T. *B-ISDN ATM Adaptation Layer—Service Specific Connection Oriented Protocol (SSCOP).* ITU-T: Q.2110, 1994.

[12] ITU-T. *B-ISDN ATM Adaptation Layer (AAL) Specification.* ITU-T Rec. I.363, 1993.

[13] ITU-T. *B-ISDN ATM Layer Cell Transfer Performance.* ITU-T Rec. I.356, 1993.

[14] ITU-T. *B-ISDN ATM Layer Specification.* ITU-T Rec. I.361, 1995.

[15] ITU-T. *B-ISDN Functional Architecture.* ITU-T Rec. I.327, 1993.

[16] ITU-T. *B-ISDN General Network Aspects*. ITU-T Rec. I.311, 1993.

[17] ITU-T. B-*ISDN Protocol Reference Model and Its Application.* ITU-T Rec. I.321, 1991.

[18] ITU-T. *B-ISDN Service Aspects.* ITU-T Rec. I.211, 1993.

[19] ITU-T. B-ISDN User-Network Interface. ITU-T Rec. I.413, 1993.

[20] ITU-T. *B-ISDN User-Network Interface—Physical Layer Specification.* ITU-T Rec. I.432, 1993.

[21] ITU-T. *B-ISDN Signalling ATM Adaptation Layer—Service Specific Coordination Function of Signalling at the User Network Interface.* (SSCF at UNI): ITU-T: Q.2130, 1994.

[22] ITU-T. *Broadband Integrated Services Digital Network (B–ISDN)—Digital Subscriber Signalling System No. 2 (DSS 2)— User-Network Interface (UNI) Layer 3 Specification for Basic Call / Connection Control.* ITU-T: Q.2931, 1995.

[23] ITU-R. *Encoding Parameters of Digital Television for Studios / Studio Encoding Parameters of Digital Television for Standard 4:3 and Wide-Screen 16:9 Aspect Ratios.* ITU-R Rec. BT. 601-4/5, gg4.

[24] Digital Audio-Visual Council. *DAVIC Specifications 1.0 and 1.1.* Digital Audio-Visual Council, 1995-1996.

[25] Teicher, D.; Herpel, C.; Schröder, E.F.; Spille, J.; and Riemann, U. "Der MPEG-2 Standard—Generische Codierung für Bewegtbilder und zugehöriger Audio-Information," *Fernseh- und Kino-Technik,* Vol. 48, Nos. 4, 5, 6, 7-8, 9, 1994.

[26] ETSI. *Digital Broadcasting Systems for Television, Sound and Data Services; Framing Structures, Channel Coding and Modulation for 11 / 12 GHz Satellite Services.* ETS 300 421, 1994.

[27] ETSI. *Digital Broadcasting Systems for Television, Sound and Data Services; Framing Structures, Channel Coding and Modulation for Cable Systems.* ETS 300 429, 1994.

[28] ETSI. *Digital Broadcasting Systems for Television, Sound and Data Services; Framing Structures, ChannelCoding and Modulation for Digital Terrestrial Television.* ETS 300 744, 1996.

[29] ISO/IEC. *Generic Coding of Moving Pictures and Associated Audio: Systems.* ISO/IEC Standard 13818-1, 1995.

[30] ISO/IEC. *Generic Coding of Moving Pictures and Associated Audio: Video.* ISO/IEC Standard 13818-2, 1995.

[31] ISO/IEC. *Generic Coding of Moving Pictures and Associated Audio: Audio.* ISO/IEC 13818-3, 1995.

[32] ISO/IEC. *Generic Coding of Moving Pictures and Associated Audio: DSM-CC.* ISO/IEC Standard 13818-6, 1995.

[33] Bhaskaran, V.; and Konstantinides, K. *Image and Video Compression Standards, Algorithms and Architectures.* Kluwer Academic Publishers: New York, 1995.

[34] ISO/IEC. *Information Technology—Coding of Moving Pictures and Associated Audio for Digital Storage Media at Up to About 1,5 Mbit/s—Part 1: Systems.* ISO/IEC Standard 11172-1, 1993.

[35] ISO/IEC. *Information Technology—Coding of Moving Pictures and Associated Audio for Media at Up to About 1.5 Mbit/s—Part 2: Video.* ISO/IEC Standard 11172-2, 1993.

[36] ISO/IEC. *Information Technology—Coding of Moving Pictures and Associated Audio for Digital Media at Up to About 1,5 Mbit/s—Part 3: Audio.* ISO/IEC Standard 11172-3, 1993.

[37] Braden, R.; Zhang, L.; Berson, S.; Herzog, S.; and Jamin, S. *Internet Draft: Resource Reservation Protocol—Version 1 Functional Specification,* 1996.

[38] Bellcore. *Local Access System Generic Requirements, objectives and Interfaces in Support of Switched Multi-megabit Data Service.* Bellcore Technical Advisory TA-TSV-000773, 1991.

[39] Wasilewski, A.J. "MPEG-2 systems specification: Blueprint for network interoperability." *Communications Technology Magazine,* February 1994.

[40] The Institution of Electrical Engineers. "MPEG-2—What It Is and What It Isn't" ELECTRONICS DIVISION Colloquium. Digest No: 1995/012.

[41] ITU-T. *OAM Principles of the B-ISDN Access*. ITU-T Rec. I.610, 1995.

[42] *Report of the Task Force on Digital Image Architecture Society of Motion Picture and Television Engineers*. White Plains, New York: 1992

[43] Braden, R.; Clark, D.; and Shenker, S. *RFC 1633: Integrated Services in the Internet Architecture: An Overview*. 1994

[44] Borden, M.; Crawley, E.; Davie, B.; and Batsell, S. *RFC 1821: Integration of Real-time Services in an IP-ATM Network Architecture*. 1995.

[45] Schulzrinne, H.; Casner, S.; Frederick, R.; Jacobson, V. *RFC 1889: RTP: A Transport Protocol for Real-Time Applications*. 1996.

[46] Schulzrinne, H. *FC 1890: RTP Profile for Audio and Video Conference with Minimal Control*. 1996.

[47] Hoffman, D.; Fernando, G.; and Goyal,V. *RFC 2038: RTP Payload Format for MPEG1 / MPEG2 Video*. 1996.

[48] ITU-T. *Synchronous Frame Structure Used at Primary and Secondary Hierachial Levels*. ITU-T Rec. G.704, 1995.

[49] ANSI. *Telecommunications—Network and Customer Installation Interfaces—Asymmetric Digital Subscriber Line (ADSL) Metallic Interface*. ANSI T1.413, 1995.

[50] ITU-T. *Traffic Control And Resource Management in B-ISDN*. ITU-T Rec. I.371, 1993.

[51] ITU-T. *Transport of MPEG-2 Constant Bit Rate Television Signals in B-ISDN.* ITU-T: J.82, 1996.

[52] ITU-T. *Transport of SDH Elements on PDH Networks: Frame and Multiplexing Structures.* ITU-T Rec. G.832, 1995.

[53] Orfali, R.; Harkey, D.; and Edwards, J. *The Essential Client / Server Survival Guide.* Wiley Computer Publishing, John Wiley & Sons, Inc.: New York, 1996.

[54] Jack, K. *Video Demystified, A Handbook for the Digital Engineer.* HighText Publications Inc., 1993.

[55] Minoli, Daniel. *Video Dialtone Technology.* McGraw-Hill, 1995.

[56] ATM Forum. *Video on Demand Specification 1.0.* ATM Forum, Technical committee, Audiovisual Multimedia Services, af-saa-0049.000, Dec. 1995,

The following is a list of figures found in this publication, which, to an extent, are based on illustrations found in ITU specifications:

Figure 6.3 partly based on ITU-T figure 9/I.363—03/93 version

Figure 4.13 partly based on ITU-T figure 6-1/I.363—03/93 version

Figure 4.14 partly based on ITU-T figure 6-5/I.363—03/93 version

Figure 4.12 partly based on ITU-T figure 1/I.363—1991 version

Figure 4.11 partly based on ITU-T figure 1/I.362—1991 version

Figure 4.9 partly based on ITU-T figure 2/I.361—1991 version

Figure 4.9 partly based on ITU-T figure 3/I.361—1991 version

Figure 4.4 partly based on ITU-T figure 1/I.321—1991 version

Figure 4.5 partly based on ITU-T figure 2/I.321—1991 version

Figure 4.10 partly based on ITU-T figure 1/I.311—1991 version

Figure 6.3 partly based on ITU-T figure 2/J.82—05/01/96 version

Figure 4.17 partly based on ITU-T figure 4-1/Q.2931—02/95 version

Figure 4.17 partly based on ITU-T figure 4-8/Q.2931—02/95 version

Appendix A: Organizations

ITU
International Telecommunication Union
Sales and Marketing Section
Place des Nations
CH-1211 Geneva 20
Switzerland
Telephone: + 41 22 730 6141
Fax: + 41 22 730 5194
E-Mail: sales@itu.ch
WWW: http://www.itu.ch

ISO/IEC
IEC Central Office
3, rue de Varembe
PO Box 131, 1211 Geneva 20
Switzerland
Telephone: + 41 22 919 02 11
Fax: + 41 22 919 03 00
E-Mail: dn@iec.ch
WWW: http://www.iec.ch

ISO Central Secretariat
1, rue de Varembré
PO Box 56, 1211 Geneva 20
Switzerland
Telephone: + 41 22 749 01 11
Fax: + 41 22 749 01 11
WWW: http://www.iso.ch

ATM Forum
The ATM Forum
2570 West El Camino Real
Suite 304
Mountain View, CA 94040-1313
USA
Telephone: + 1 415 949 6700
Fax: + 1 415 949 6705

ATM Forum, *continued*
E-Mail: info@atmforum.com
WWW: http://www.atmforum.com

Audio Engineering Society

Audio Engineering Society Inc.
East 42nd Street,
Room 2520,
New York NY 10165-2520
USA
Telephone: + 1 212 661 8528
Fax: + 1 212 661 7829
WWW: http//www.aes.org/

DAVIC

DAVIC Secretariat
Mr. Nicola Bellina
Strada Antica di Collegno, 253
I-10146 Torino
Italy
Telephone: + 39 11 7720 111
Fax: + 39 11 725 679
E-Mail: nicola.bellina@davic.it
WWW: http://www.davic.org

DVB
DVB Project Office
European Broadcasting Union
Case Postal 67—17A Ancienne Route
CH-128 Grand-Saconnex (Geneva)
Switzerland
Telephone: + 41 22 717 27 19
Fax: + 41 22 717 27 27
E-Mail: dvb@pax.eunet.ch
WWW: http://www.dvb.org

IETF
IETF Secretariat
c/o Corporation for National Research Initiatives
1895 Preston White Drive, Suite 100
Reston, VA 20191-5434
USA
Telephone: +1 703 620 8990
Fax: +1 703 758-5913
E-Mail: ietf-info@ietf.org
WWW: http://www.ietf.org

The Institution of Electrical Engineers

Michael Faradays House

Six Hills way

Stevenage

Herts, SG1 2AY

UK

Telephone: + 44 171 240 1871

Fax: +44 171 240 7735

WWW: http://www.iee.org.uk

Appendix B:
List of Acronyms

AAL ATM Adaptation Layer
The ATM adaptation layer helps to map service layer data into ATM cells. Depending on the requirements of the service, different adaptation layers can be used.

ADSL Asymmetric Digital Subscriber Line
A technology that exploits the existing twisted pair telephone wiring network to deliver high speed services to the consumer over short distances. Various modulation schemes such as DMT and CAP are used to achieve high bandwidth.

ATM Asynchronous Transfer Mode
The data transfer and multiplexing method, defined as the fundament for B-ISDN. The ATM technology allows integration of video, data, and voice information as

required, on the same transmission media. ATM is independent of the physical layer and does not, in principle, have any limit in bandwidth.

AU   Access Unit
In MPEG, an Access Unit is basically a block of data that when decoded, becomes a presentation unit as, for instance, a picture.

B-ICI   Broadband Inter Carrier Interface
The ATM Forum specification for public Network-to- Network Interface (NNI) signalling

B-ISDN   Broadband Integrated Service Digital Network
The vision of a single integrated network carrying different kinds of services including audio, video, and data.

B-ISUP   Broadband ISDN User Part
ITU-T specification for public Network-to- Network Interface (NNI) signalling.

CA   Conditional Access
In MPEG, the term to restrict the access to a program by means of encryption.

CAP   Carrierless Amplitude Phase modulation
Modulation scheme used typically in the access network, for instance the FTTC scenario. Via phase modulation, it is possible for instance to transmit bitrates in excess of 50 Mbps via twisted pair copper cables. (Phase modulation: Bits are represented via a number of pre-defined phase conditions.)

CDV   Cell Delay Variation
Also referred to as Cell Clumping; the situation where the time between the arrival of one cell and the next cell varies.

CIF   Common Interchange Format
A set of parameters defining the picture size and picture rate. CIF was defined to allow video phone applications to exchange video picture.

CLP   Cell Loss Priority
A bit in the ATM cell header, indicating the relative importance of the cell.

CORBA   Common Object Request Broker Architecture
The object model defined by the Object Management Group. DSM-CC User-to-User is utilizing the CORBA model.

COFDM   Coded Orthogonal Frequency Division Multiplexing
Multicarrier modulation technique used in terrestrial broadcast systems carrying digital video.

CS   Convergence Sublayer
The convergence sublayer of some of the ATM adaptation layers are split into a common part (Common Part Convergence Sublayer) and a service specific part (SSCS).

CPCS   Common Part Convergence Sublayer
All services using a specific AAL can use the functionality of the CPCS. This can be CRC checks and length indications.

CPS   Content Provider System
In the DAVIC specification, the term for systems and equipment belonging to the content provider, including encoding and network systems.

dB   Decibel
A way of representing signal levels on a logarithmic scale relative to a specific reference value.

DCT   Discrete Cosine Transform
The transformation method used to convert a signal from the time into the frequency domain. Used by the audio and video compression process in MPEG.

DMT   Discrete Multi-Tone modulation
Modulation technique used in ADSL. Utilizes phase modulation techniques in several frequency bands simultaneously with transmit information. (Phase modulation: Bits are represented via a number of pre-defined phase conditions.)

DS   Delivery System
In DAVIC, all the (network) equipment used to a Service Provider System with a Consumer System.

DSM-CC   Digital Storage Medium Command and Control
A set of protocols defined by MPEG to control and manage the flow of video information.

DSRM   DAVIC System Reference Model
An overall model to describe the different entities building a multimedia system and the interfaces between them.

DTS   Decode Time Stamp

A time stamp telling the decoder at what time to decode a video or audio access unit.

ES   Elementary Stream

A sequence of video or audio access units encoded according to MPEG; can also contain user defined data.

FEC   Forward Error Correction

A technique that protects the PDUs transmitted over the network from bit errors/loss. On the transmission side, a certain amount of overhead information is added and calculated via a specific technique, for instance the R/S (Reed-Solomon). On the receiving side, the PDUs are checked against the FEC information and possible bit errors/loss is corrected.

FFT   Fast Fouirer Transformation

A way of transforming time domain signals into the frequency domain with high accuracy. Used as part of the MPEG audio compression process.

FTTB,
FTTH   Fiber to the Building, Fiber to the Home

An access network architecture where a fiber cable is deployed to the consumer's home or office building. An in-house network then distributes the information to the end user.

FTTC   Fiber to the Curb

An access network architecture where fiber is deployed to a central point relatively close to the consumer. The last part to the consumer is then covered by coax or twisted pair copper media organized in a star topology.

GFC   Generic Flow Control
A field in the ATM header that can be used to carry flow control information. Present only at the user-network interface (UNI)

GOP   Group of Pictures
In MPEG a number of pictures that are grouped together to form a logical unit. Starts with an Intracoded (I-) picture.

HDSL   High Speed Digital Subscriber Line
A technology that exploits the existing twisted pair telephone wiring network in order to deliver high speed services to the consumer. HDSL provides transmission in both directions at rates typically lower than ADSL.

HEC   Header Error Control
A field for a CRC checksum in the ATM cell header, used to protect the first four bytes of the cell header. The correlation between the HEC field and the first four header bytes also allows the receiving equipment to identify the cell boundaries.

HFC   Hybrid Fiber Coax
Similar to Fiber to the Curb, HFC is an access network technology where fiber and copper are used in a mixed architecture. The copper part is typically an existing cable TV coax network. Due to the topology of cable TV networks, the return channel access to the HFC is shared between the users.

IDCT   Inverse Discrete Cosine Transform
The inverse function of the DCT. IDCT is used to transfer the image or audio information back from the frequency domain to the time domain.

IDL   Interface Definition Language
A description language that is used to describe interfaces in a distributed environment.

IE   Information Element
IEs are included in the B-ISDN UNI signalling messages. The IE can carry information on the called or calling number, the QoS requested for the connection, and the AAL used.

IP   Internetwork Protocol
A widely used protocol to interconnect systems and networks.

ISDN   Integrated Service Digital Network
A narrowband network that is used to transport different services, for instance voice, data, and low quality video. Also known as N-ISDN or Narrowband ISDN.

LFE   Low Frequency Enhancement channel
Optional channel available in MPEG-2 audio. Carries low frequency information used for special effects.

LMDS   Local Multipoint Distribution System
A wireless access network technology using microwave transmission in both the downstream and upstream directions.

MMDS   Multichannel Multipoint Distribution System
A wireless access network technology using microwave transmission in the downstream direction. The upstream information can be carried via the POTS.

MPEG   Moving Pictures Experts Group
A sub-working group of the ISO/IEC defining standards for the coding and handling of moving pictures and associated audio information.

MPTS   Multi Program Transport Stream
A transport stream carrying multiple programs.

NBC   Non-Backwards Compatible
MPEG-2 and MPEG-1 audio is to a far extent compatible. However, work is being done on an MPEG-2 audio specification that has no compatibility with MPEG-1 audio in order to achieve more efficient compression.

N-ISDN   Narrowband ISDN
See ISDN

NIT   Network Information Table
A data structure in MPEG-2 systems carrying information about the network transporting the MPEG-2 data. Typically used by the network provider to transport network related information.

NNI   Network Node Interface
The interface between networks. ATM cells transmitted via this interface have a different format than ATM cells at the interface between user and network. Also, the signalling happening at the NNI is different compared to the one happening at the UNI.

NTSC   National Television Standard Committee
An analog video standard originated and used in the US and some other countries in the Americas.

OAM   Operation And Maintenance
Procedures and PDU structures used to monitor and manage the B-ISDN network. At the ATM level, special OAM ATM cells exist to monitor the QoS and the path/channel availability.

OMG   Object Management Group
A group of companies and institutes working on the standardization of object-oriented processing in a distributed environment, e.g., a network.

OMG-CDR   OMG Common Data Representation
The data representation format chosen by the OMG.

ONU   Optical Network Unit
Distribution point in the access network.

ORB   Object Request Broker
The central entity in the CORBA model allowing transparent access to distributed functions in a network.

OSI   Open System Interconnection
A protocol reference model defined by ISO describing the functionality of network protocols via seven layers. The OSI model contains the following layers: physical, link, network, transport, session, presentation, and application layer. The OSI model is generally used as conceptual reference in the telecommunication and data communication environment

PAL   Phase Alternate Line
An analog video standard primarily used in Europe and Asia.

PAT   Program Association Table
A data structure in MPEG-2 systems providing the initial information about which programs are transported in the current MPEG-2 transport stream.

PCI   Protocol Control Information
See PDU

**PCR
(MPEG)**   Program Clock Reference
A time stamp provided in the MPEG-2 transport stream that is used to adjust the decoder clock

**PCR
(ATM)**   Peak Cell Rate
The maximum number of cells per time period on a specific virtual channel.

PDH   Plesiochronous Digital Hierarchy
A telecommunication technology presently being used all over the world. PDH is based on Time Division Multiplexing (TDM) but can carry also ATM cells. In North America, typical rates are 1.5 Mbps DS-1 and 45 Mbps DS-3. In Europe, 2 Mbps E1 and 34 Mbps E3 are predominant.

PDU   Protocol Data Unit
A "block" of data seny from a transmitter to a receiver. The protocol implementations in the transmitter and receiver are encoding and decoding the PDU according to a given PDU specification. A PDU for layer N contains a SDU

from the layer above (N+1) plus additional Protocol Control Information (PCI) from layer N. Via the PCI, the layer N on the transmitting side can communicate with layer N on the receiving side.

PES   Packetized Elementary Stream
An elementary stream that is divided into variable length packets. The header of each packet provides additional information to process the stream.

PID   Packet Identifier
A field in the header of the transport packet header structure identifies packets that belong together. Is also used to identify the content of the packet.

PMD   Physical Media Dependent
The lower sublayer of the physical layer. Describes, among other things, pulse shapes, amplitude levels, and line encoding used in the physical media.

PMT   Program Map Table
A data structure in MPEG-2 systems carrying information about which transport packets are forming a program.

P-NNI   Private NNI
ATM Forum specification for Network-to-Network Interface (NNI) signalling on private premises.

POTS   Plain Old Telephone System
The public service telephone system, as we know it today.

PRBS   Pseudo Random Bit Sequence
A pre-defined bit sequence appearing "random" used to measure bit error rate.

PSI   Program Specific Information
The collection of tables such as the Program Association Table, Program Map Table, Conditional Access Table, and Network Information Table.

PSTN   Public Service Telephone Network
The public telephone system, as we know it today used for voice communication.

PTI   Payload Type Indicator
A field in the ATM cell header to describe the ATM cell payload. It is used in ATM Adaptation Layer Type 5 to indicate the end of AAL 5 PDU.

PTS   Presentation Time Stamp
A time stamp indication of when the decoded data should be presented to the user.

QAM   Quadrature Amplitude Modulation
Modulation technique widely used in coaxial cable systems carrying digital video and based on phase modulation. (Bits are represented via a number of pre-defined phase conditions)

QoS   Quality of Service
The quality of service of a communication link is given by a set of parameter values, describing the delay between transmitter and receiver or the maximum number of bit errors tolerable on the communication link.

QPSK   Quarternary Phase Shift Keying
Modulation technique widely used for instance in satellite systems carrying digital video and based on phase modulation.

RGB   Red, Green, Blue

A color space describing a color by splitting it up into its red, green, and blue components.

RPC   Remote Procedure Call

In a software application, a RPC is a method to call a function that is implemented on a remote system.

SAR   Segmentation And Reassembly

A sublayer of the AAL. Performs the segmentation of the CS PDUs into ATM cells on the transmitting side, and the reverse function on the receiving side. Can contain additional information, such as sequence numbers and time stamps, depending on the AAL.

SCR   System Clock Reference

The equivalent to the Program Clock Reference, but in an MPEG program stream.

SDH   Synchronous Digital Hierarchy

Add-drop multiplexing-based transmission method used to carry ATM cells over long distances. Is considered as the replacement for the PDH network presently installed. Originally standardized by the CCITT in 1988 on the basis of the SONET specifications. Predominant in Europe.

SDU   Service Data Unit

See PDU

SECAM   Sequentiel Couleur Avec Mémoire

Analog video standard developed in France and now used in some African countries.

SIF   Standard/Source Interchange/Input Format

A digital video format used in MPEG-1 video.

SMR   Signal to mask ratio

A term describing the difference in magnitude of the actual audio signal and the magnitude of the noise that is just imperceptible to the human ear in a given frequency band. The SMR is used in audio compression techniques in order to determine the number of bits needed to describe the audio samples.

SNMP   Simple Network Management Protocol

A widely accepted network management protocol, typically used in private and enterprise networks.

SNR   Signal to Noise Ratio

The ratio between the magnitude of the actual signal and the "disturbing signal" (noise).

SONET   Synchronous Optical NETwork

Add-drop multiplexing-based transmission method used to carry ATM cells over long distances. Is considered as the replacement for the PDH network presently installed. Predominant in North America.

SPS   Service Provider System

In DAVIC, all the equipment used at the service provider premise to deliver a service to the consumer.

SPTS   Single Program Transport Stream

A transport stream carrying several PES streams, referring all to the same time base and forming a program.

SSCF   Service Specific Convergence Function
Translation function used to adopt the UNI/NNI signalling protocols to the SSCOP.

SSCOP   Service Specific Connection Oriented Protocol
A mechanism that offers assured delivery of the signalling messages. (The signalling protocols assume the messages as successfully transmitted, as the AAL does not offer guaranteed delivery.)

SSCS   Service Specific Convergence Sublayer
A part of the CS in some AALs allowing adaptation to a specific service, additional to what the CPCS can offer. May not be used and is then referred to as "Null."

STB, STT,
STU   Settop Box, Settop Terminal, Settop Unit
A device at the consumer premise, decoding the delivered data.

STM   Synchronous Transfer Module
Hierarchy levels/transmission frame structure of the SDH transmission method. STM-1 consist of a frame size of 2430 bytes, which is transmitted with a frequency of 8 KHz, yielding a bit rate of 155 Mbps.

STS   Synchronous Transport Module
Hierarchy levels/transmission frame structure of the SONET transmission method. The lowest level is STS-1 at a bit rate of 52 Mbps.

TCP   Transmission Control Protocol
A widely used protocol providing a reliable data transfer between transmitting and receiving parties.

TDM   Time Division Multiplexing
A method of multiplexing utilizing time slots. One or more times/second the user can transmit a specified amount of data. Utilized in PDH.

U-N   User-to-Network
A part of the MPEG-2 DSM-CC standard dealing with the interface between user (video server or set top box) and the delivery network.

U-U   User-to-User
A part of the MPEG-2 DSM-CC standard dealing with the interface between user (video server or set top box) and the delivery network.

UNI   User-to-Network Interface
In B-ISDN, the User-to-Network interface connects the user equipment, typically a terminal or PC, to the public network.

VBV   Video Buffering Verifier
A hypothetical model of a video decoder used to verify that an encoded bit stream would not cause buffer overflow or underflow in a real decoder

VCC   Virtual Channel Connection
A logical connection between a transmitter and a receiver in an ATM network, identified by a pair of VCI and VPI numbers.

VCI   Virtual Channel Identifier
A number identifying a logical channel within a virtual path in an ATM network.

VDSL   Very High Speed Digital Subscriber Line
Access network technology allowing transport of 52 Mbps
of downstream information over short distances of twisted pair copper cable. Utilizes the CAP modulation scheme.

VPI   Virtual Path Identifier
A number identifying a path in an ATM network.

YCrCb   A colorspace defined by the ITU-R, describing a color by a
luminance (Y) and two chrominance (Cr and Cb) compo-
nents.

Index